SHORT EYES

SHORT EYES

A PLAY BY
MIGUEL PIÑERO

A MERMAID DRAMABOOK
Hill and Wang New York
A DIVISION OF FARRAR, STRAUS AND GIROUX

Library of Congress Cataloging in Publication Data

Piñero, Miguel.
Short eyes.

(A Mermaid dramabook)
I. Title.
PS3566.I5216S5   1975   812'.5'4   75-2080
ISBN 0-8090-8659-X
ISBN 0-8090-12324 pbk.

Dedicated to the power of Adelina Piñero-Rivera

Adelina de Gurabo
es una mujer que le
dió diez potencias a la
nación puertorriqueña.
Adelina, Adelina
Adelina, Adelina
brought out to
the world the
true energy
she creates Dusmic Energy
she does not sell a bill
of lies to bring about
a revolution: no she dances
beyond that: Nuyorican is a
state of mind,
it is a metaphysics
of being
and Adelina
brought ten beauties
to the world of pain.
She put muscles on the planet

she bore children for the
freedom of the world
she used no
ploys
she used a truth that
creates men of feelings
and power & aggression
it is a noble mind
it is a full, giving
powerful loving mind
that Adelina gives
New York.

Excerpt from "El Cumpleaños de Adelina," a poem
by Miguel Algarin

INTRODUCTION

It seems like only yesterday that Miguel Piñero spoke to me about one of several plays he was writing. He seemed more pleased with *Short Eyes* than with any of his other plays. We had met in Sing Sing (where I was working as an actor-in-residence and assistant to Mr. Clay Stevenson) in the spring of 1972. By early summer of 1973 we had developed a friendship in which little thought was given to the fact that we were living in different worlds: mine, the free world; his, the prison.

We considered several projects that never got off the ground or through the bars. Our only successful project while Miky was incarcerated was winning an award for one of his poems, "Black Woman with the Blonde Wig On." I submitted the poem to a contest while working as Special Programs Consultant to the Council on the Arts in Westchester County. The poem won an award and I almost won a little vacation in the "joint" with Miky. In the May 27, 1971, issue of *The New York Times,* Mel Gussow had reviewed our show *Prison Sounds,* which included "Black Woman with the Blonde Wig On," and in recognition of Miky's promise he acknowledged his poetic ability and mentioned the poetry award. The warden at Sing Sing read Gussow's article, called us into his office, and read us the Riot Act. He called it contraband. I called it good poetry.

While Sing Sing was producing a corps of writers, the Bedford Hills Correctional Facility was giving birth to a troupe of actors. This was the germ of The Family. It was a difficult and lonely task to work with these men, and each time they opened the gate for me at the Bedford Hills prison I felt compelled to give the best that was in me. I discovered several things as I proceeded to work, and before long I realized that discipline and continuity were missing from the prisoners' lives and that these were the things that theater could give to a group of men who, for the most part, had nothing to look forward to but a release date, forty dollars, and a suit.

The workshop at Bedford Hills started out with conventional theatrical exercises. When we invented new exercises, the guys began to approach me about the possibility of performing. Jimmy Beasley and Vincent Rivera, our playwrights-in-residence, supplied us with original material combined with writings ranging from those of James Weldon Johnson to those of Felipe Luciano. Together we created *New York, New York, the Big Apple,* a series of monologues and improvisations. This theater piece made some definite changes in the atmosphere of the prison and the quality of life of several men doing their "bid" in a hopeless world. The changes have extended far beyond those prison walls and manifested themselves in a theater workshop called The Family. I remember Kenny Steward, two months short of release, asking me: "Pancho man, like you got me into this shit and like, man, I'm hooked on this theater thing, so what the fuck is we gonna do when I get out, man?" There were many answers to that, but the words I spoke came to me from my teacher, the mother of us all, Doña Vinnette Carroll: "Darling, the secret ingredient of success is hard work." And that has become the gospel for The Family today.

The name "The Family," along with our first production in "the street world" (the outside world), was inspired by Colleen Dewhurst and a group of citizens who recognized the great talent behind bars at Bedford Hills. Polly Siwek, Joan Potter, Roy Potter, Constance Clayton, Lawrence Beal Smith, Winn Smith, Maria Sobol, Roy Poole, Molly Bliss, Liz Berger, and Jackie Blount were among the supporters of The Family.

I met men at the gate as they were released and brought them from a prison slave system to a Manhattan workshop that they themselves created; and so they could avoid the cold, hard existence that had faced them so many times before. Instead of going back to the block or a kind of situation that could lead them back to jail, they went to a workshop to rehearse. Work was the operative word. We met and worked and worked until everybody was exhausted. Often there was no money for food or carfare, but somehow we managed to scrape up something for the night or the next day's rehearsal. Work was beginning to take on real meaning. Commitment was heavy. We were working in the Players' Workshop on the Lower East Side, which the actors had been known to walk to from as far away as Harlem. My studio apartment in Manhattan served as a refuge for whoever needed it. At some point every member of The Family had taken me up on my invitation: "Esta es tu casa." We knew where to find each other, and in the early stage of our existence the fear of turning the corner and being picked up on a "humble" (any misdemeanor that could land someone back in jail) or looking backward and finding ugly temptation chasing us was on everybody's mind. It was not uncommon to be awakened by the telephone or the doorbell at any hour by someone feeling he was being led astray who needed to be "delivered from evil." Corny as it sounds, it worked. In spite of the obstacles, we found a way to make it happen.

Our first production was *New York, New York, the Big Apple*. With this play, we performed in schools, colleges, and churches from northern Westchester County down to Scarsdale. We traveled with a good artistic reputation, little money, and the strongest kind of desire imaginable to remain together as a theatrical "family."

Ms. Dewhurst alerted her friends in the theater that new blood was coming their way. Ted Mann invited us to use his rehearsal space. I knew that my feeling about artists from prison making a new life as actors, playwrights, and musicians was right.

Just before Miky's release from Sing Sing, he got a five-day furlough and got the chance to see The Family at work. He decided that these people were having an experience he wanted to share. Arthur Bartow, Director of Theatre at the Riverside Church, had read Mel Gussow's article commenting on Piñero's work, and he offered Miky a job at the church. Miky then hired me as his unpaid consultant. The Family left the Players' Workshop and became a resident company at the church.

When Miky showed us his draft of the first act of *Short Eyes,* we were not surprised at the depth and beauty of the piece. When the question of doing *Short Eyes* came up, it was the easiest decision in the world.

It was important for the members of The Family that they discover that you could get a better high off of your creativity than off of any of those cold, unnatural, deadly chemicals that they were addicted to, and that they be recognized as serious actors who happened to come from unfortunate circumstances.

We worked together and approached *Short Eyes*—even before it was completed—as if it were a masterpiece, a total experience; and even today we think of it in this way.

First we had to do some outside casting, which was foreign to us. We operate on an open-door policy; outsiders can come in and work with us. All we looked for was desire and commitment. But when we were suddenly faced with judging someone else's talent, we were frightened. Getting past the difficult experience of casting allowed the real work to begin.

We sat and read the play until the actors couldn't take it any more. But by the time we were ready to block it, everyone was enthusiastic. Changing structure in the play, improvising, bringing life to the words became a thing of joy. There were times when it looked like it was not going to happen; some of us became discouraged. But the thing that kept all of us going was a feeling of unity and of having a stake in creating the play.

Before the end of the three-week run at the Riverside Church, David Eidenberg of the Public Theater had been urged by Colleen Dewhurst to see the play. She had also contacted Joseph Papp.

From the Riverside Church to the Public Theater, from the Annenberg Center in Philadelphia to Lincoln Center in New York City, from Holland and Germany to Hartford, Connecticut, from the New York Drama Critics Award to two Obies and various other awards and prizes and citations, from forty-seven dollars a week to five hundred dollars a week, from the worst review to the most sensational review, we continued—under every new physical, emotional, or financial condition—to see the play as a new experience. Adjustments, changes, and discoveries meant much to us, who wished to re-create life in warm, honest, and beautiful terms. I imagine we put in the kind of rehearsal time put into an old Moscow Theater production of *The Cherry Orchard* or a great musical composition by Tito Puente.

I urge the readers of *Short Eyes* not to search for some great social reform message or to analyze the personal motives of the original cast or to fall into the trap of feeling this play can be done only by ex-inmates or people from a subculture. Read it as a play that can and should be acted by any serious-minded group of people wishing to do a play that appeals to them.

Miguel Piñero is no more a playwright because he went to jail than Tennessee Williams is a playwright because he came from the South. Tito Goya (Cupcakes) is not a "sweet kid," Ben Jefferson (Ice) never masturbated to Jane Fonda's picture, and J. J. Johnson (El Raheem) has never been a Muslim or a porter. When the prisoners enter the dayroom, we are witnessing not a prison play but a play about human relationships.

We see Omar, a perennial prisoner, doing his bid, being concerned primarily about "getting on the help" so he can benefit from the extra cigarettes or whatever little goodies he can get from the commissary and, of course, the favors others render him—especially the "sweet kids" (those considered "stuff").

Murphy, the tough Irishman, becomes tougher in order to survive in a world of Puerto Ricans and blacks, where he controls the flow of drugs and homemade wine inside the "joint." Murphy has more resentment for the alleged child rapist, Clark Davis, than anyone else in the prison.

Clark Davis represents an emotionally disturbed man from an emotionally disturbed society. His death is the result of the rigidity of social values and morals in the prison world, because the values we witness in the play are the same as those of the outside world, but more intensified. Prison is a society within a society, and Clark Davis's life and death are the result of both societies. Juan's judgment of Davis's death in his rap to Cupcakes is meant to reach the other participants in Davis's murder, as well as everyone in the theater audience: "You blew it because you placed yourself above understanding." Juan is the outlaw who makes no excuses.

Paco is the dope fiend and *bugarrón,* the *payaso,* moving with quick, loud, tropical rhythms, laughing on the outside while he searches for love to help him through his bid. "Willing to go both ways," he even makes an unsuccessful attempt to conquer Cupcakes sexually.

Cupcakes is our youth, our hope, and very vulnerable because of his own fears. But at the same time he enjoys all the attention that he receives from the other love-starved prisoners. His beauty and innocence become their shot of dope.

El Raheem represents a search for self through an original religion. He is definitely not a Muslim or a Black Panther. He is a man choosing to do his bid by studying and teaching *his* truth about the original black man. His not being able to kill someone "looking up at me helpless" is not an act of cowardice but a very touching element of humanity.

When the critics reviewed the audience's reaction to the play as well as the play itself, we all knew that we were involved in something more than a prison drama or a slice of life by an ex-convict. We were involved in a human story. Miguel Piñero, this "saintly outlaw," this *espiritista* of words, has given birth to a play that has poetry which can be trusted and respected.

MARVIN FELIX CAMILLO

New York City
December 1974

CAST
(in alphabetical order)

MR. BROWN	Hollis Barnes
SERGEANT MORRISON	Chuck Bergansky
JUAN OTERO	Bimbo
CHARLIE "LONGSHOE" MURPHY	Joseph Carberry
CLARK DAVIS	William Carden
JULIO "CUPCAKES" MERCADO	Tito Goya
JOHN "ICE" WICKER	Ben Jefferson
WILLIAM "EL RAHEEM" JOHNSON	J. J. Johnson
BLANCA	Chu Chu Malave
MR. FREDERICK NETT	Robert Maroff
GYPSY	Rick Reid
OMAR BLINKER	Kenny Steward
PACO PASQUAL	Felipe Torres
CAPTAIN ALLARD	H. Richard Young

The play was directed by Marvin Felix Camillo, with sets designed by David Mitchell, costumes designed by Paul Martino and supervised by David Mitchell, and lighting by Spencer Mosse. Producer, Joseph Papp; Associate Producer, Bernard Gersten.

Short Eyes was first produced by the Theatre of the Riverside Church. There it was seen by Joseph Papp, who took it to his Anspacher Theater and then, after a two-week run at the Zellerbach Theater in Pennsylvania, to the Vivian Beaumont Theater at Lincoln Center, where it opened as part of the New York Shakespeare Festival on May 9, 1974, with the above cast.

SHORT EYES

THE PEOPLE

JUAN   *A Puerto Rican in his early thirties*

CUPCAKES   *A Puerto Rican pretty boy of twenty-one who looks younger*

PACO   *A Puerto Rican in his early thirties with the look of a dope fiend*

ICE   *A black man in his late twenties who looks older*

OMAR   *A black amateur boxer in his mid-twenties, virile*

EL RAHEEM   *A black man in his mid-twenties with regal look and militant bearing*

LONGSHOE   *A hip, tough Irishman in his mid-twenties*

CLARK DAVIS   *A handsome, frightened white man in his early twenties*

MR. NETT   *An old-line white prison guard in his late forties*

CAPTAIN ALLARD   *Officer in House of Detention. Straight and gung-ho*

MR. BROWN   *An officer in the House of Detention*

SERGEANT MORRISON   *Another officer*

BLANCA *and* GYPSY   *Walk-on, nonspeaking parts*

The entire play takes place in the dayroom on one of the floors in the House of Detention.

ACT I: *Early morning, lock-in after breakfast*
ACT II: *Same day at 3:00 p.m.*
EPILOGUE: *Same evening*

ACT ONE

Dayroom in the House of Detention. Upstage right is entrance gate. Upstage left is gate leading to shower room and slop sink. Upstage center is a toilet and drinking fountain. Above is a catwalk. Stage left is a table and chairs. Downstage right is a garbage can. Upstage right is a TV set on a stand. Early-morning lock-in after the morning meal.

Early-morning light.

INMATES' VOICES *can be heard: various ad-libs, calling out to each other, asking questions, exchanging prison gossip, etc.*

MORRISON
All right, listen up . . . I said listen up.
(*Whistle*)
When I call your names, give me your cell location.
(*Catcalls*)
Off the fucking noise. Now if I have to call out your name more than once, pray—cause your soul may belong to God, but your ass is mine.

(*More catcalls. House lights go out*)
Williams, D.

VOICE RESPONSE
Upper D 14.

MORRISON
Homer, J.

VOICE RESPONSE
Lower D 7.

MORRISON
Stone, F.

VOICE RESPONSE
Lower D 5.

MORRISON
Miller, G.

VOICE RESPONSE
Upper D 3.

MORRISON
Lockout for criminal court . . .
(*Whistle*)
"A" side dayroom. All right, already! . . . knock it off.
Supreme Court.
(*Whistle*)
Johnson.

INMATE VOICE
Who?

MORRISON
Johnson.

TWO INMATE VOICES
Who?

MORRISON
Johnson.

A LOT OF VOICES
Who? . . . who? . . . who? . . . who? . . .

MORRISON
Aw, come on, fellas, give me a break.

INMATE VOICE
Your brains may belong to the state, but your sanity belongs to me.

INMATE VOICE
Aw, come on, fellas, give the fella a break.

INMATE VOICE
Break . . .
(*Bronx cheer*)

MORRISON
Johnson.

INMATE VOICE
Upper D 15.

MORRISON
Corree-a.

INMATE VOICE
Can't you say my name right?
(*Giving proper pronunciation*)
Correa . . . Correa . . . Correa.

MORRISON
You guys go to the "C" side dayroom
(*Whistle*)
Sing Sing reception center. Gomez, A.

VOICE RESPONSE
Lower D 9.

MORRISON
Shit-can-do.
(*Catcalls*)

VOICE RESPONSE
Scicando . . . Lower D 11.

MORRISON
Bring all your personal belongings and go to the "B" side
dayroom.
(*Catcalls*)
All right, you guys want to play games, you guys don't let
up that noise, you guys ain't locking out this morning.

INMATE VOICE
You got it.
(*Ad-libs continue until* OMAR *speaks*)

ICE
Fuck you, sucker.
(*Silence. Sound of prison gate opening is heard*)

MORRISON

(*Whistle—dayroom lights come on*)
All right, on the lockout.
(*Enter* OMAR, LONGSHOE, EL RAHEEM, PACO, *and* ICE. *Each
runs toward his respective position. Ad-libs.*
   Then JUAN *walks slowly toward his position.*
   CUPCAKES *is the last to come in. The* MEN *accompany
him with simple scat singing to the tune of "The Stripper."
Ad-libs*)

JUAN

Why don't you cut that loose? Man, don't you think that
kid get tired of hearing that every morning?

PACO

Oh, man, we just jiving.

ICE

Hey, Cupcake, you ain't got no plexes behind that, do you?

CUPCAKES

I mean . . . like no . . . but . . .

PACO

You see, Juan, Cupcake don't mind.

CUPCAKES

No, really, Juan. Like I don't mind . . . But that doesn't
mean that I like to listen to it. I mean . . . like . . . hey
. . . I call you guys by your name. Why don't you call me
by mine? My name ain't Cupcakes, it's Julio.

EL RAHEEM

If you would acknowledge that you are God, your name

wouldn't be Cupcake or Julio or anything else. You would be Dahoo.

LONGSHOE
All ready! Can't you spare us that shit early in the a.m.?

EL RAHEEM
No . . . one . . . is . . . talking . . . to . . . you . . . Yacoub.

LONGSHOE
The name is Longshoe Charlie Murphy . . . *Mister* Murphy to you.

EL RAHEEM
Yacoub . . . maker and creator of the devil . . . swine merchant. Your time is near at hand. Fuck around and your time will be now. Soon all devils' heads will roll and now rivers shall flow through the city—created by the blood of Whitey . . . Devil . . . beast.

OMAR
Salaam Alaikum.

PACO
Salami with bacons.

ICE
Power to the people.

LONGSHOE
Free the Watergate 500.

JUAN
Pa'lante.

CUPCAKES
Tippecanoe and Tyler too.

PACO
(*On table, overly feminine*)
A la lucha . . . a la lucha . . . que somo mucha . . .

OMAR
Hey! Hey . . . you know the Panthers say "Power to the people."

MR. NETT
On the gate.

OMAR
(*Strong voice*)
Power to the people. And gay liberators say . . .
(*High voice, limp wrist in fist*)
Power to the people.
(*Enter* NETT)

MR. NETT
How about police power?

JUAN
How about it? Oink, oink.

MR. NETT
Wise guy. Paco, you got a counsel visit.

PACO

Vaya.

OMAR

Mr. Nett?

MR. NETT

Yeah, what is it?

OMAR

Mr. Nett, you know like I've been here over ten months—and I'd like to know why I can't get on the help. Like I've asked a dozen times . . . and guys that just come in are shot over me . . . and I get shot down . . . Like why? Have I done something to you? Is there something about me that you don't like?

MR. NETT

Why, no. I don't have anything against you. But since you ask me I'll tell you. One is that when you first came in here you had the clap.

OMAR

But I don't have it any more. That was ten months ago.

MR. NETT

How many fights have you had since the first day you came on the floor?

OMAR

But I haven't had a fight in a long time.

MR. NETT

How many?

OMAR

Seven.

MR. NETT

Seven? Close to ten would be my estimation. No, if I put you on the help, there would be trouble in no time. Now if you give me your word that you won't fight and stay cool, I'll give it some deep consideration.

OMAR

I can't give you my word on something like that. You know I don't stand for no lame coming out the side of his neck with me. Not my word . . . My word is bond.

EL RAHEEM

Bond is life.

OMAR

That's why I can't give you my word. My word is my bond. Man in prison ain't got nothing but his word, and he's got to be careful who and how and for what he give it for. But I'll tell you this, I'll try to be cool.

MR. NETT

Well, you're honest about it anyway. I'll think it over.
(PACO *and* MR. NETT *exit*)

EL RAHEEM

Try is a failure.

OMAR

Fuck you.

EL RAHEEM
Try is a failure. Do.

OMAR
Fuck you.

EL RAHEEM
Fuck yourself, it's cheaper.

CUPCAKES
Hey, Mr. Nett—put on the power.

MR. NETT
(*From outside the gate*)
The power is on.

CUPCAKES
The box ain't on.

MR. NETT
Might be broken. I'll call the repairman.

JUAN
Might as well listen to the radio.

ICE
The radio ain't workin' either, Juan. I tried to get BLS a
little while ago and got nothin' but static, Jack.

CUPCAKES
Anyone wants to play Dirty Hearts? I ain't got no money,
but I'll have cigarettes later on this week.

OMAR
Money on the wood makes bettin' good.

ICE

Right on.
(LONGSHOE *gives* CUPCAKES *cigarettes*)

JUAN

Hey, Julio.
(*Throws* CUPCAKES *cigarettes.*
  BROWN *appears outside entrance gate*)

BROWN

On the gate.
(*Gate opens and* PACO *enters. Gate closes and* BROWN *exits*)

CUPCAKES

Shit. That was a real fast visit.

PACO

Not fast enough.

LONGSHOE

What the man say about your case?

PACO

The bitch wants me to cop out to a D—she must think
my dick is made of sponge rubber. I told her to tell the
D.A. to rub the offer on his chest. Not to come to court on
my behalf—shit, the bitch must have made a deal with the
D.A. on one of her paying customers. Man, if I wait I
could get a misdemeanor by my motherfucking self. What
the fuck I need with a Legal Aid? Guess who's on the
bench?

ICE

Who they got out there?

PACO

Cop-out Levine.

ICE

Wow! He give me a pound for a frown.

PACO

First they give me a student, and now a double-crossin'
bitch.

LONGSHOE

We all got to make a living.

PACO

On my expense? No fucking good.

EL RAHEEM

You still expect the white man to give you a fair trial in
his court? Don't you know what justice really means?
Justice . . . "just us" . . . white folks.

PACO

Look here, man. I don't expect nothing from nobody—
especially the Yankees. Man, this ain't my first time before
them people behind these walls, cause I ain't got the
money for bail. And you can bet that it won't be my last
time—not as long as I'm poor and Puerto Rican.

CUPCAKES

Come on, let's play . . . for push-ups.

JUAN

How many?

CUPCAKES

Ten if you got just one book, fifteen if you got two.

PACO

I ain't playing for no goddamn push-ups.

ICE

Hey—come on, don't be like that.

PACO

Said ain't playing for no push-ups. Tell you what, let's play for coochie-coochies.

ICE

What the hell is coochie-coochies?

JUAN

It's a game they play in Puerto Rico. You ever see a flick about Hawaii? Them girls with the grass skirts moving their butts dancing? That's coochie-coochies.

ICE

I thought that was the hula-jack.

PACO

Put your shirt on your hips like this and move your ass. Coochie-coochie-coochie . . .

CUPCAKES

That's out.

PACO

You got a plexes?

CUPCAKES

Told you before that I don't have no complexes.

JUAN

You got no plexes at all?

CUPCAKES

No.

JUAN

Then why not let me fuck you?

CUPCAKES

That's definitely out.

JUAN

People without complexes might as well turn stuff.

OMAR

Thinking of joining the ranks? Cruising the tearooms?

EL RAHEEM

What kind of black original man talk is that? Cupcakes puts the wisdom before the knowledge because that's his nature. He can't help that. But you are deliberately acting and thinking out of your nature . . . thinking like the white devil, Yacoub. Your presence infects the minds of my people like a fever. You, Yacoub, are the bearer of three thousand nine hundred and ninety-nine diseases . . . corrupt . . . evil . . . pork-chop-eating brain . . .

LONGSHOE

Look.

EL RAHEEM

Where?

LONGSHOE

I'm sick and . . .

EL RAHEEM

See, brothers, he admits he is sick with corruption.

LONGSHOE

Who?

EL RAHEEM

You're not only the devil, you're also an owl?

LONGSHOE

Why?

EL RAHEEM

"Y"—why? Why is "Y" the twenty-fifth letter of the alphabet?

LONGSHOE

You . . . son of . . .

EL RAHEEM

You . . . me . . . they . . . them. This . . . those . . . that . . . "U" for the unknown.

LONGSHOE

I . . . I . . .

EL RAHEEM

Eye . . . I . . . Aye . . . Aye . . . Aiiii . . . hi . . .

LONGSHOE
Games, huh?

EL RAHEEM
The way of life is no game. Lame.

LONGSHOE
G . . . O . . . D . . . D . . . O . . . G . . . God
spelled backward is dog . . . dog spelled backward is God
. . . If Allah is God, Allah is a dog.

EL RAHEEM
Allah Akbar.
(*Screams, jumps on him*)
Allah Akbar.
(MR. NETT *and* BROWN *appear outside entrance gate*)

MR. NETT
On the gate.
(BROWN *opens gate.* MR. NETT *and* BROWN *enter.* MR. NETT
breaks them apart)

MR. NETT
What the hell is going on here?

OMAR
Mr. Nett, let these two git it off, else we's gonna have
mucho static around here.

ICE
Yeah . . . Mr. Nett . . . they got a personality thing
going on for weeks.

MR. NETT
Fair fight, Murphy?

LONGSHOE
That's what I want.

MR. NETT
Johnson?

EL RAHEEM
El Raheem. Johnson is a slave name.
(*Nods*)
May your Christian God have mercy on your soul, Yacoub.
(BROWN *closes gate.*
   EL RAHEEM *and* LONGSHOE *square off and begin to fight
. . . boxing . . . some wrestling.*
   LONGSHOE *is knocked clean across the room*)

LONGSHOE
Guess you say that left hook is Whitey trickology?

EL RAHEEM
No, honky, you knocked me down. My sister hits harder
than that. She's only eight.
(*They wrestle until* EL RAHEEM *is on top. Then* NETT
breaks them apart)

OMAR
Why didn't you break it up while Whitey was on top?

MR. NETT
Listen, why don't you two guys call it quits—ain't none of
you really gonna end up the winner . . . Give it up . . .
be friends . . . shake hands . . . Come, break it up, you
both got your shit off . . . break it up. Go out and clean
yourselves up. Make this the last time I see either of you
fighting. On the gate. Next time I turn on the water.
(BROWN *and* NETT *exit, gate closes.*

The RICANS *go to their table and begin to play on the table as if it were bongos)*

ICE
You two got it together.

EL RAHEEM
I am God . . . master and ruler of my universe . . . I am always together.

OMAR
Let me ask you one question, God.

EL RAHEEM
You have permission to ask two.

OMAR
Thank you . . . If you're God, why are you in jail? God can do anything, right? Melt these walls down, then create a stairway of light to the streets below . . . God. If you're God, then you can do these things. If you can't, tell me why God can't do a simple thing like that.

EL RAHEEM
I am God . . . I am a poor righteous teacher of almighty Allah and by his will I am here to awaken the original lost in these prisons . . . Black original man is asleep . . . This is your school of self-awareness. Wake up, black man, melt these walls? You ask me, a tangible god, to do an intangible feat? Mysterious intangible gods do mysterious intangible deeds. There is nothing mysterious about me. Tangible gods do tangible deeds.
(PUERTO RICAN GROUP *goes back to playing. "Toca, si, va, tocar")*

CUPCAKES

(*On table, M.C.-style*)

That's right, ladies and gentlemen . . . damas y caba-
lleros . . . every night is Latin night at the House of
Detention. Tonight for the first time . . . direct from his
record-breaking counsel visit . . . on congas is Paco
Pasqual . . . yeaaaaaa. With a all-star band . . . for your
listening enjoyment . . . Juan Bobo Otero on timbales
. . . On mouth organ Charles Murphy . . . To show you
the latest dancing are Iceman, John Wicker . . . and his
equally talented partner, Omar Blinker . . . yeaaaaaa.
While tapping his toes for you all . . . moving his head
to the rhythm of the band is the mighty El Raheem,
yeaaaaaaa. Boooooooo. Yes, brothers and sisters, especially
you sisters, don't miss this musical extravaganza. I'll be
there, too . . . to say hello to all my friends . . . So be
there . . . Don't be the one to say "Gee, I missed it" . . .
This is your cha-cha jockey, Julio . . .

ALL

Cupcakes . . .

CUPCAKES

Mercado . . . Be sure to be there . . . Catch this act . . .
this show of shows before they leave on a long extended
touring engagement with state . . .
(PACO *pinches* CUPCAKES's *ass*)
Keep your hands off my ass, man.
(CUPCAKES *moves stage left, sits pouting. Ad-libs*)

PACO

Hey, kid, do one of those prison toasts . . .
(*They urge him on with various ad-libs*)

CUPCAKES

All right, dig . . . You guys gotta give me background
. . . Clap your hands and say . . . Mambo tu le pop . . .
It was the night before Christmas . . . and all through
the pad . . . cocaine and heroin was all the cats had. One
cat in the corner . . . copping a nod . . . Another
scratching thought he was God . . . I jumps on the phone
. . . and dial with care . . . hoping my reefer . . . would
soon be there . . . After a while . . . crowding my style
. . . I ran to the door . . . see what's the matter . . .
And to my surprise . . . I saw five police badges ·. . .
staring . . . glaring in my eyes . . . A couple of studs
. . . starts to get tough, so I ran to the bathroom . . . get
rid of the stuff . . . narc bang . . . bang . . . but they
banged in vain . . . cause you see . . . what didn't go in
my veins went down the drain . . . Broke down the door
. . . knock me to the floor . . . and took me away, that's
the way I spent my last Christmas Day . . . like a dirty
dog . . . in a dark and dingy cell . . . But I didn't care
cause I was high as hell . . . But I was cool . . . I was
cool . . . I was cool . . . You people are the fools . . .
cream of the top . . . cause I got you say something as
stupid as Mambo tu le pop.
(GROUP *chases* CUPCAKES *around stage.*

BROWN *and* CLARK DAVIS *appear outside entrance gate*)

BROWN

On the gate.
(*Gate opens and* CLARK DAVIS *enters, goes to stage center.*
BROWN *closes gate and exits*)

CUPCAKES

Hey, Longshoe . . . one of your kin . . . look-a-like sin
just walked in . . .

EL RAHEEM

Another devil.

LONGSHOE

Hey . . . hey, whatdayasay . . . My name's Longshoe Charlie Murphy. Call me Longshoe. What's your name?

CLARK

Davis . . . Clark . . . Ah . . . Clark Davis . . . Clark is my first name.

PACO

Clark Kent.

CUPCAKES

Mild-mannered, too.

OMAR

No, no, Superman.
(*Other ad-libs: "Faster than a speeding bullet," etc.*)

PACO

Oye . . . Shoe . . . Está bueno . . . Pa' rajalo . . .

LONGSHOE

Back . . . back . . . boy . . . no está bueno . . . anyway, no mucho . . . como Cupcake.

PACO

Vaya.

LONGSHOE

Pay them no mind . . . crazy spics . . . where you locking?

CLARK

Upper D 15.

LONGSHOE

Siberia, huh? . . . Tough.

CLARK

First time in the joint.

LONGSHOE

Yeah? Well, I better hip you to what's happening fast.

ICE

Look out for your homey, Shoe.

OMAR

Second.

LONGSHOE

Look here, this is our section . . . white . . . dig? That's the Rican table, you can sit there if they give you permission . . . Same goes with the black section.

ICE

Say it loud.

OMAR

I'm black and proud.

ICE

Vaya!

LONGSHOE

Most of the fellas are in court. I'm the Don Gee here. You

know what that mean, right? Good . . . Niggers and the
spics don't give us honkies much trouble. We're cool half
ass. This is a good floor. Dynamite hack on all shifts. Stay
away from the black gods . . .
(NETT *appears outside gate*)

NETT
On the gate.

LONGSHOE
You know them when you see them.
(NETT *opens gate and enters*)

NETT
On the chow.

ICE
What we got, Mr. Nett?

NETT
Baloney à la carte.

ICE
Shit, welfare steaks again.
(*All exit except* CLARK *and* LONGSHOE. *Gate stays open. The
men reenter with sandwiches and return to their respective
places.*
    NETT *closes gate and exits*)

LONGSHOE
Black go on the front of the line, we stay in the back . . .
It's okay to rap with the blacks, but don't get too close with
any of them. Ricans too. We're the minority here, so be
cool. If you hate yams, keep it to yourself. Don't show it.

But also don't let them run over you. Ricans are funny people. Took me a long time to figure them out, and you know something, I found out that I still have a lot to learn about them. I rap spic talk. They get a big-brother attitude about the whites in jail. But they also back the niggers to the T.

ICE
(*Throws* LONGSHOE *a sandwich*)
Hey, Shoe.

LONGSHOE
If a spic pulls a razor blade on you and you don't have a mop wringer in your hands . . . run . . . If you have static with a nigger and they ain't no white people around . . . get a spic to watch your back, you may have a chance . . . That ain't no guarantee . . . If you have static with a spic, don't get no nigger to watch your back cause you ain't gonna have none.

OMAR
You can say that again.

ICE
Two times.

LONGSHOE
You're a good-looking kid . . . You ain't stuff and you don't want to be stuff. Stay away from the bandidos. Paco is one of them . . . Take no gifts from no one.
(NETT *appears outside entrance gate*)

NETT
Clark Davis . . . Davis.

CLARK
Yes, that's me.

NETT
On the gate.
(NETT *opens gate, enters with* CLARK's *belongings, leaves gate open*)
Come here . . . come here . . . white trash . . . filth . . . Let me tell you something and you better listen good cause I'm only going to say it one time . . . and one time only. This is a nice floor . . . a quiet floor . . . There has never been too much trouble on this floor . . . With you, I smell trouble . . . I don't question the warden's or the captain's motive for putting you on this floor . . . But for once I'm gonna ask why they put a sick fucking degenerate like you on my floor . . . If you just talk out the side of your mouth one time . . . if you look at me sideways one time . . . if you mispronounce my name once, if you pick up more food than you can eat . . . if you call me for something I think is unnecessary . . . if you oversleep, undersleep . . . if . . . if . . . if . . . you give me just one little reason . . . I'm gonna break your face up so bad your own mother won't know you . . .

LONGSHOE
Mr. Nett is being kinda hard . . .

NETT
Shut up . . . I got a eight-year-old daughter who was molested by one of those bastards . . . stinking sons of bitches and I just as well pretend that he was you, Davis, do you understand that . . .

PACO
Short eyes.

LONGSHOE

Short eyes? Short eyes . . . Clark, are you one of those
short-eyes freaks . . . are you a short-eyes freak?

NETT

Sit down, Murphy . . . I'm talking to this . . . this scum-
bag . . . yeah, he's a child rapist . . . a baby rapist, how
old was she? How old? . . . Eight . . . seven . . . Dis-
gusting bastard . . . Stay out of my sight . . . cause if
you get in my face just one time . . . don't forget what
I told you . . . I'll take a night stick and ram it clean up
your asshole . . . I hope to God that they take you off
this floor, or send you to Sing Sing . . . The men up there
know what to do with degenerates like you.

CLARK

I . . . I . . .

NETT

All right, let's go . . . Lock in . . . lock in . . . for the
count . . . Clark, the captain outside on the bridge wants
to see you. I hope he takes you off this floor . . .

LONGSHOE

Hey, Davis . . .
(*Walks up to him and spits in his face.*
Men exit)

NETT

Juan, stay out and clean the dayroom. Omar, take the tier.
(CAPTAIN ALLARD *appears on the catwalk above.* CLARK *joins*
ALLARD *and they carry on inaudible conversation.*
Crossing from stage right to stage left on the catwalk

are CUPCAKES, ICE, *and* LONGSHOE, *followed by* MR. BROWN. *As* LONGSHOE *passes, he bumps* CLARK.

  MR. BROWN *stops beside* CLARK, *and* CAPTAIN ALLARD *chases after* LONGSHOE *to catwalk above left*)

ALLARD

Hey, just a minute, you. That's just the kind of stuff that's going to cease.
(BROWN *and* CLARK *exit catwalk above right and appear at entrance gate stage right*)

BROWN

On the gate.
(BROWN *opens gate,* CLARK *enters dayroom,* BROWN *closes gate.* CLARK *says something inaudible to* BROWN)
You're lucky if you get a call before Christmas.
(BROWN *exits.* CLARK *leans on gate*)

LONGSHOE

Get off that fuckin' gate.
(*While the above was going on,* JUAN *has taken his cleaning equipment from the shower upstage left and placed can of Ajax and rag on the toilet area upstage center, and broom, mop, bucket, dustpan, dust broom, dust box in downstage left corner.* JUAN *sits at table,* CLARK *at window.* JUAN *pours coffee, offers* CLARK *a sandwich.* CLARK *crosses to table and sits*)

JUAN

Hey, man, did you really do it?
(OMAR *starts chant offstage*)

CLARK

I don't know.

JUAN

What do you mean, you don't know? What you think I am, a fool, or something out of a comic book.

CLARK

No . . . I don't mean to sound like that, I . . . I . . .

JUAN

Look, man, either you did it or you didn't.
(JUAN *stands*)
That all there is to it . . .

CLARK

I don't know if I did it or not.

JUAN

You better break that down to me
(*Sits*)
cause you lost me.

CLARK

What I mean is that I may have done it or I may not have . . . I just don't remember . . . I remember seeing that little girl that morning . . . I sat in Bellevue thirty-three days and I don't remember doing anything like that to that little girl.

JUAN

You done something like that before, haven't you?

CLARK

I . . . ye . . . yes . . . I have . . . How did you know?

JUAN

Your guilt flies off your tongue, man.

(*Stands*)

Sound like one of those guys in an encounter session
(*Starts to sweep*)
looking to dump their shit off on someone . . . You need
help . . . The bad part about it is that you know it . . .

CLARK

Help? I need help? Yes . . . yes, I do need help . . . But
I'm afraid to find it . . . Why? . . . Fear . . . just fear
. . . Perhaps fear of knowing that I may be put away
forever . . . I have a wife and kid I love very much . . .
and I want to be with them. I don't ever want to be away
from them . . . ever. But now this thing has happened
. . . I don't know what to do . . . I don't know . . . If I
fight it in court, they'll end up getting hurt . . . If I
don't, it'll be the same thing . . . Jesus help me . . .
God forgive me.

JUAN

Cause man won't.
(JUAN *at downstage left corner sweeping up dust*)

CLARK

No, man won't . . . Society will never forgive me . . . or
accept me back once this is openly known.
(JUAN *begins to stack chairs stage right.* CLARK *hands* JUAN
a chair)
I think about it sometimes and . . . funny, I don't really
feel disgusted . . . just ashamed . . . You wanna . . .

JUAN

Listen to you? It's up to you . . . You got a half hour
before the floor locks out unless you wanna go public like
A.A.
(JUAN *picks up stool*)

CLARK

No . . . no . . . no . . . I can't . . . I didn't even talk
with the psychiatrist in the bughouse.

JUAN

Run it . . .
(JUAN *puts down stool*)

CLARK

You know, somehow it seems like there's no beginning.
Seems like I've always been in there all my life. I have like
little picture incidents running across my mind . . . I
remember being . . . fifteen or sixteen years old
(JUAN *crosses upstage center to clean toilet*)
or something around that age, waking up to the sound of
voices coming from the living room . . . cartoons on the
TV . . . They were watching cartoons on the TV, two
little girls. One was my sister, and her friend . . . And
you know how it is when you get up in the morning, the
inevitable hard-on is getting up with you. I draped the
sheet around my shoulders . . . Everyone else was sleeping . . . The girl watching TV with my sister . . .
yes . . . Hispanic . . . pale-looking skin . . . She was
eight . . . nine . . . ten . . . what the difference, she was
a child . . . She was very pretty—high cheekbones, flash-
ing black eyes . . . She was wearing blue short pants . . .
tight-fitting . . . a white blouse, or shirt . . . My sister
. . . she left to do number two . . .
(JUAN *returns to stage right*)
She told her friend wait for me, I'm going to do number
two, and they laughed about it. I sneaked in standing a
little behind her . . . She felt me standing there and
turned to me . . . She smiled such a pretty little smile

. . . I told her I was a vampire and she laughed . . . I spread the sheets apart and she suddenly stopped laughing . . . She just stood there staring at me . . . Shocked? surprised? intrigued? Don't know . . . don't know . . . She just stood and stared . . .

(JUAN *crosses to downstage left*)

I came closer like a vampire . . . She started backing away . . . ran toward the door . . . stopped, looked at me again. Never at my face . . . my body . . . I couldn't really tell whether or not the look on her face was one of fear . . . but I'll never forget that look.

(BROWN *crosses on catwalk from left to right with a banana. Stands at right*)

I was really scared that she'd tell her parents. Weeks passed without confrontation . . . and I was feeling less and less afraid . . . But that's not my thing, showing myself naked to little girls in schoolyards.

(JUAN *crosses to downstage right corner and begins to mop from downstage right to downstage left*)

One time . . . no, it was the first time . . . the very first time. I was alone watching TV . . . Was I in school or out . . . And there was this little Puerto Rican girl from next door . . . Her father was the new janitor . . . I had seen her before . . . many times . . . sliding down the banister . . . Always her panties looked dirty . . . She was . . . oh, why do I always try to make their age higher than it really was . . . even to myself. She was young, much too young . . . Why did she come there? For who? Hundred questions. Not one small answer . . . not even a lie flickers across my brain.

OFFSTAGE VOICE

All right, listen up. The following inmates report for sanitation duty: Smalls, Gary; Medena, James; Pfeifer,

Willis; Martinez, Raul. Report to C.O. grounds for sanitation duty.

CLARK
How did I get to the bathroom with her? Don't know. I was standing there with her, I was combing her hair. I was combing her hair. Her curly reddish hair . . .
(JUAN *crosses upstage right, starts to mop upstage right to upstage left*)
I was naked . . . naked . . . except for these flower-printed cotton underwears . . . No slippers, barefooted . . . Suddenly I get this feeling over me . . . like a flash fever . . . and I'm hard . . . I placed my hands on her small shoulders . . . and pressed her hand and placed it on my penis . . . Did she know what to do? Or did I coerce her? I pulled down my drawers . . . But then I felt too naked, so I put them back on . . . My eyes were closed . . . but I felt as if there was this giant eye off in space staring at me . . .
(JUAN *stops upstage left and listens to* CLARK, *who is unaware* JUAN *is in back of him*)
I opened them and saw her staring at me in the cabinet mirror. I pulled her back away from the view of the mirror . . . My hands up her dress, feeling her under-developed body . . . I . . . I . . . I began pulling her underwear down on the bowl . . . She resisted . . . slightly, just a moment . . . I sat on the bowl . . . She turned and threw her arms around my neck and kissed me on the lips . . . She gave a small nervous giggle . . . I couldn't look at her . . . I closed my eyes . . . turned her body . . . to face away from me . . . I lubricated myself . . . and . . . I hear a scream, my own . . . there was a spot of blood on my drawers . . . I took them off right then and there . . . ripped them up and flushed

them down the toilet . . . She had dressed herself up and asked me if we could do it again tomorrow . . . and was I her boyfriend now . . . I said yes, yes . . .

(JUAN *goes to center stage, starts mopping center stage right to stage left.*

BROWN *exits from catwalk above right*)

I couldn't sit still that whole morning, I just couldn't relax. I dressed and took a walk . . . Next thing I know I was running—out of breath . . . I had run over twenty blocks . . . twenty blocks blind . . . without knowing . . . I was running . . . Juan, was it my conscious or subconscious that my rest stop was a children's playground . . . Coincidence perhaps . . . But why did I run in that direction, no, better still, why did I start walking in that direction . . . Coincidence? Why didn't my breath give out elsewhere . . . Coincidence?

(JUAN *moves to downstage left,* CLARK *moves to upstage center and sits on window ledge*)

I sat on the park bench and watched the little girls swing . . . slide . . . run . . . jumprope . . . Fat . . . skinny . . . black . . . white . . . Chinese . . . I sat there until the next morning . . . The next day I went home and met the little Puerto Rican girl again . . . Almost three times a week . . . The rest of the time I would be in the playground or in the children's section of the movies . . . But you know something? Er, er . . .

(CLARK *moves toward* JUAN, *who is in downstage left corner*)

JUAN

Juan.

CLARK

Yes, Juan . . . Juan the listener . . . the compassionate

. . . you know something, Juan . . . I soon became . . . became . . . what? A pro? A professional degenerate?
(*The sound of garbage cans banging together is heard off-stage*)
I don't know if you can call it a second insight on children. But . . . I would go to the park . . . and sit there for hours and talk with a little girl and know if I would do it or not with her . . . Just a few words was all needed . . . Talk stupid things they consider grownup talk . . . Soon my hand would hold hers, then I would caress her face . . . Next her thighs . . . under their dress . . . I never took any of them home or drove away with them in my car . . . I always told them to meet me in the very same building they lived in . . .

OFFSTAGE VOICE
On the sanitation gate.
(*Sound of gate opening*)

CLARK
On the roof or their basements under the stairs . . . Sometimes in their own home if the parents were out . . . The easiest ones were the Puerto Ricans and the black girls . . . Little white ones would masturbate you right there in the park for a dollar or a quarter . . . depending on how much emphasis their parents put in their heads on making money . . . I felt ashamed at first . . . But then I would rehearse at nights what to do the next time . . . planning . . . I
(JUAN *starts moving slowly from downstage left to upstage left*)
couldn't help myself . . . I couldn't help myself . . . Something drove me to it . . . I thought of killing myself . . . but I just couldn't go through with it . . . I don't

really wanna die . . . I wanted to stop, really I did . . . I just didn't know how. I thought maybe I was crazy . . . but I read all types of psychology books . . . I heard or read somewhere that crazy people can't distinguish right from wrong . . . Yet I can . . . I know what's right and I know what I'm doing is wrong, yet I can't stop myself . . .

JUAN

Why didn't you go to the police or a psychiatrist . . .
(JUAN *crosses to shower room upstage left*)

CLARK

I wanted to many a time . . . But I know that the police would find some pretext to kill me . . . And a psychiatrist . . . well, if he thought he couldn't help me he'd turn me over to them or commit me to some nut ward . . . Juan, try to understand me.
(JUAN *comes out of shower room and starts putting away his cleaning equipment*)

JUAN

Motherfucker, try to understand you . . . if I wasn't trying to, I would have killed you . . . stone dead, punk . . .
(JUAN, *at downstage left corner, picks up broom and bucket*)
The minute you said that thing about the Rican girls . . . If I was you I'd ask transfer to protection . . . cause
(JUAN *returns to shower room*)
if you remain on this floor you're asking to die . . . You'll be committing involuntary suicide . . .
(JUAN *again crosses to downstage left corner, picks up remaining equipment, crosses to toilet, picks up Ajax and rag, and crosses to shower room*)

Shit, why the fuck did you have to tell me all of it . . .
You don't know me from Adam . . .
(JUAN *comes out of shower room and crosses to* CLARK,
stage center)
Why the hell did you have to make me your father con-
fessor? Why? Why didn't you stop, why?

CLARK

Cause you asked. Cause you . . . What I told you I didn't
even tell the doctors at the observation ward . . . Everything is coming down on me so fast . . . I needed to tell
it all . . . to someone . . . Juan, you were willing to
listen.
(*Whistle blows*)

MR. NETT
(*Offstage*)
All right, on the lockout . . .
(*Whistle*)

OTHER VOICES
On the lockout.
(BROWN *appears outside the gate*)

BROWN
On the gate.
(*Enter* EL RAHEEM, PACO, OMAR, ICE, CUPCAKES, *and* LONG-
SHOE. BROWN *closes gate and exits.* ICE *and* OMAR *get one
chair and cross to table.* OMAR *starts playing cards.*
LONGSHOE *gets his stool and crosses to behind table.*
CUPCAKES *does push-ups on chair stage right*)

ICE
You're gonna be on the help for good, Omar.

OMAR

No, the man said just for today . . . But he put me on top of the list.

ICE

You gonna look out for me, heavy homeeeeey?

OMAR

Since when did we become homeeeeeys? Shit, man— you're way out there in Coney Island somewhere . . . and I'm way in Bed-Stuy.

ICE

How you gonna show, brother man? It's the same borough, ain't it?

OMAR

It's the same borough, Iceman . . . but it's a different world.

ICE

Ain't this a bitch? I comes on this here floor with this man . . . There was nothing but Whiteys on the floor. It was me and him against the world . . . I come out every night and stand by his side, ready to die . . . to die . . .

PACO

Yeah, cause you no wanna die alone.

ICE

That has nothing to do with nothing.

OMAR

It has everything to do with everything.

ICE

How you going to show? How you do this to me, Omar, homey.

OMAR

Being how you mentioned it, perhaps it's not a bad idea. Save me some money when you go to the store.

ICE

I ain't gonna argue that . . . cause this is me, the Iceman, talking—my hand don't call for this type of talking, man. Your main mellow-man, this is too strong . . . Contracts . . .

OMAR

Who said anything about contract? I didn't say anything about contract . . . Anybody here said anything about a contract? . . .

CUPCAKES

I didn't hear anybody say anything . . . I didn't say it.

PACO

Me neither . . .

LONGSHOE

Who could say anything with a swollen lip.

JUAN

I mind my own business.

OMAR

See, you must be hearing things.

ICE

You didn't say it . . . but you implied it . . . You was
leading right up to it.

OMAR

Well, now that you mentioned it . . . perhaps it's not a
bad idea . . .

ICE

How you gonna do this to me? Omarrrrr . . . homeeey . . .

OMAR

Did it to yourself . . . You knew I'd always look out . . .
but now you put these ideas into my head . . . and it
sounds kinda . . .

ICE

Omar . . . my pretty nigger . . . even if you get no
bigger, you'll always be my main nigger . . . And if you
get any bigger, you'll just be my bigger nigger . . .

OMAR

Better run that shit on the judge . . . You know what you
can do for me . . . give me a softshoe.

ICE

Yes sir, boss, captain, your honor, mister, sir.
(*Fast softshoe*)

OMAR

Hey, freak.
(*To* CLARK)
You're sittin' on my Chinese handball court . . .
(CLARK *moves to upstage right*)

ICE

That there is where I hangs my wet clean clothes . . .
and I don't wanna have them sprayed. Move . . . creep.
(CLARK *moves to stage center*)

EL RAHEEM

You're in God's walking space.
(CLARK *moves to lower stage right*)

PACO

That's Paco's walking space.

CUPCAKES

Hey, Clark . . . that spot's not taken . . . Right over
there . . . Yeah, that's right . . . The whole toilet bowl
and you go well together.

CLARK

I'm not going to stand for this treatment.

PACO

Did you say something out of your mouth, creep . . .

OMAR

You talking to everyone, or to someone in particular?

LONGSHOE

I know you ain't talking to me.

ICE

You got something you wanna say to someone in this room,
faggot?

CLARK

I was talking to myself.

EL RAHEEM

Well, don't talk to yourself too loud.

CUPCAKES

Talk to the shitbowl . . . You'll find you got a lot in common with each other . . .

JUAN

Drop it . . . Cut it loose . . .

PACO

¿Donde está La Mancha? . . . or did Sancho go to another floor? . . .

JUAN

Paco . . . one of these days you gonna get me very very angry.

PACO

I'm trembling, man . . . whooo, I'm scared . . . Can't you smell it, I'm shitting bricks . . .

ICE

Juan . . . be cool . . . don't know why you wanna put front for that freak . . . But, man . . . if you don't wanna vamp . . . don't go against your own people . . . You be wrong, man . . .

JUAN

Ain't going against my own brother man . . . But if the dude is a sicky . . . cut him loose . . . All that ain't necessary . . . Ice.

ICE

It ain't your place, Juan, and you know it . . . You're out of time . . .

PACO
I think he has a special interest.

ICE
Don't come out of your face wrong, Paco.

PACO
Ice.

ICE
You're interrupting me, Paco . . . Me and you both know where you're coming from . . . Don't make me put your shit in the streets . . . And, Juan, you know you're out of order. This ain't your turn, man . . .

CUPCAKES
Let's go do up them clothes, Juan.

JUAN
Yeah. O.K., kid . . . go get the buckets . . . I'll be down the tier.
(BROWN *appears outside gate*)

CUPCAKES
On the gate.

BROWN
On the gate.
(BROWN *opens gate and* CUPCAKES *and* JUAN *exit.* BROWN *closes gate and exits*)

PACO
Man thinks he El grande Pingú . . .

ICE

Squash it . . .

LONGSHOE

(*Goes over to toilet, where* CLARK *is*)

Hey, man . . . don't leave. I want you to hold it for me
. . . while I pee.

CLARK

What . . . wha . . .

LONGSHOE

I want you to hold my motherfucking dick while I pee,
sucker, so I don't get my hands wet . . .

(*Laughter*)

Well?

CLARK

No . . . no . . . I can't do that . . .

LONGSHOE

Oh. You can't do that . . . but you can rape seven-year-old
girls.

CLARK

I didn't rape anybody. I didn't do anything.

LONGSHOE

Shut up, punk.

(*Pushes* CLARK's *chest*)

What's this—smokes.

CLARK

They're all I have . . . but you're welcome to some.

LONGSHOE
Some? I'm welcome to all of them, creep.

CLARK
What about me?

LONGSHOE
What about you?

CLARK
They're all I have.

LONGSHOE
Kick.

CLARK
But . . .

ICE
Kick, motherfucker, kick.

LONGSHOE
Kick . . . hey, let me see that chain . . . gold . . .

CLARK
Yes.

LONGSHOE
How many carats?

CLARK
Fourteen.

ICE
Damn, Shoe . . . if you gonna take the chain, take the
chain.

LONGSHOE

I . . . me . . . take . . . Who said anything about taking anything. That would be stealing and that's dishonest, ain't it, Clarky baby . . . You wanna give that chain, don't you . . . After all, we're both white and we got to look out for one another. Ain't that true, Clarky baby . . . You gonna be real white about the whole thing, aren't you, Clarky baby.

CLARK

It's a gift from my mother.

ALL

Ohhh.

LONGSHOE

I didn't know you had a mother . . . I didn't think human beings gave birth to dogs, too.

OMAR

Looks like the freak ain't upping the chain, Shoe.

LONGSHOE

Oh man, Clarky baby, how you gonna show in front of these people? You want them to think we're that untogether? What are you trying to say, man? You mean to stand there in your nice cheap summer suit looking very white and deny my whiteness by refusing to share a gift with me? That totally uncool . . . You're insulting me, man.

OMAR

Man's trying to say that you're not white enough.

LONGSHOE

You're trying to put a wire out on me, creep?

OMAR

Man saying you're a nigger-lover.

LONGSHOE

You saying that I'm a quadroon?

EL RAHEEM

What? Freak, did you say that devil has some royal Congo blood in his veins?

ICE

I ain't got nothin' to do with it, Shoe, but I swore I heard the freak say that you were passing, Shoe.

CLARK

I didn't say that . . . I didn't say anything.

ICE

You calling me a liar.

CLARK

No, no . . . no.

LONGSHOE

Then you did say it?
(*They all push* CLARK *around*)

CLARK

Please, please, here, take this chain, leave me alone.

ICE

(*Yanks chain from around neck*)
Pick the motherfucking chain up, freak.

EL RAHEEM

That's right . . . You tell that man he ain't good enough to talk to.

LONGSHOE

First I'm a nigger-lover . . . then a quadroon . . . Now I'm not even good enough to talk to.

EL RAHEEM

Boy, I told you about being in God's walking space, didn't I?

ICE

You better answer God when he speaks, boy.

LONGSHOE

Don't you turn your back on me, motherfucker.
(*Strikes* CLARK. *He falls against* EL RAHEEM, *who hits him too.*
OMAR *begins kicking him.*
MR. NETT *appears outside gate*)

MR. NETT

On the gate.
(NETT *opens gate, enters*)

OMAR

Mr. Nett.

EL RAHEEM

Mr. Nett, Mr. Nett, the man started a fight with Omar and we just broke it up.

ICE

That's right, Mr. Nett.

MR. NETT

You guys shouldn't whip his face. Omar, you are on the help permanently. The Torres brothers beat their case this morning.

OMAR

Right on . . . Bet them two are high as all hell by now.

MR. NETT.

Yeah, and they'll be back, mark my words . . . Listen, get this man off the floor . . . You guys know the rules . . . No sleeping on the floor.
(MR. NETT *closes gate and exits*)

ICE

You guys oughta learn how to touch up a dude.

OMAR

I'll get a bucket of water.

LONGSHOE

Fuck the bucket of water, Omar. Put the sucker's head in the toilet bowl. There's water there.

EL RAHEEM

He's still a devil . . . I won't do that to no man.

LONGSHOE

We could get it on again.

EL RAHEEM

That don't present me no problems . . .

ICE

Squash it, man . . . both of you . . .

LONGSHOE

Come on, Omar, grab his other side . . .

OMAR

Hey, there's still piss in there.

LONGSHOE

Put his head in and I'll flush it.

EL RAHEEM

Omar . . . let me put his head in there and you flush it.

LONGSHOE

Makes me no difference . . . flush the motherfucker, Omar.

(OMAR, LONGSHOE, PACO *pick up* CLARK *to put his head in toilet bowl. They use him as a ramrod, making three runs at the toilet,* CLARK *screaming. On third ram, toilet is flushed, and lights fade*)

ACT TWO

Same scene. Half an hour later. JUAN *is playing chess with* ICE. PACO *is seated at table, watching* ICE *and* JUAN *play chess.* OMAR *and* CUPCAKES *are doing exercises.* EL RAHEEM *is writing, talking to himself.* LONGSHOE *is reading.*

ICE

You know, it's kinda like a shame what these dudes did to that poor ugly misbegotten son of a bitch. I feel almost sorry for the slob. They do that to me or even think of doing it . . . it's war . . . to the bitter end.

JUAN

Spare me . . . Where they take him?

ICE

Don't know . . . don't care . . . and don't give a fuck . . .

OMAR

They took him down for P.I. . . .

CUPCAKES

Pi?

OMAR

Positive Identification . . . stupid.

CUPCAKES

Your mama.

OMAR

My mama don't play that shit . . . and neither do I . . .

EL RAHEEM

I hope they don't bring him back on the floor . . .

JUAN

Who, Short Eyes?

EL RAHEEM

Yeah . . . I got the feeling . . . and the knowledge working full and I feel it . . .

ICE

Feel what, man?

JUAN

You know as well as I do what . . . Go on, it's your play . . .

ICE

Looks like you made the wrong move there, governor . . . it seems that I am going to have to prove to you young whippersnapper that you can't fool around with an old man . . .

JUAN

You sure talk a lotta shit, Ice.

ICE

You're in check, my good fellow—chip, chip, cheerios and all that shit . . . Ten months, and I finally beat that motherfucker.

LONGSHOE

I hear you talking, Ice . . . git em . . .

ICE

Excuse me, my good man, while I answers nature's call . . . I shall return shortly . . . Motherfucker, you better not cheat . . . Let me cop that heist when you're through . . . Shoe.

LONGSHOE

You're on it second . . . Cupcakes cracked already.

EL RAHEEM

I don't understand you niggers, sometimes . . . Here you got an opportunity to learn about yourselves . . . about the greatness of the black man. And what you do? . . . Spend your time reading filthy books . . . talking negative shit . . . beating your meat at night . . . Nothing that'll benefit you in the future world of the black man . . . The time for the devil is almost up . . . He was meant to rule for a certain time and his time is near, almost too near.

LONGSHOE

El, let me tell you something. I'm a hope-to-die dope fiend . . . not cause I'm black . . . or cause I have some personality disorder, but because I like being a dope fiend. I like being a dope fiend. And nothing is gonna change that in me . . . If Allah comes down from wherever he is . . .

and he ain't doing good dope . . . I ain't gonna cop from him . . . And I'll put out a wire that his thing is cut with rat poison . . . Why don't you go back into your lessons and git off my motherfucking back . . . Cause I do as I please when the day comes that I wanna become a black god, a Panther or a Muslim, then I will become one . . . Right now all this shit you keep running about us being niggers—stupid and ignorance ain't gonna get you nothing but a good kick in the ass . . .

ICE
(*Continuing*)
Let me cop that heist, Cupcake—

CUPCAKES
When you gonna learn that I'm número uno.

OMAR
Come on, número uno . . . do me número ten push-ups—

PACO
Uno, do, tre, quatro . . .

OMAR
Hey, will you look at this. What kinda push-ups are those suppose to be—his ass all up in the air.

PACO
El culito está cojiendo ire.

CUPCAKES
I hope Geraldo Rivera gives you the shock of your life.

OMAR
Weak—weak.

LONGSHOE
Better get some friends to burn some candles for you.

PACO
Corny little guy, ain't he?

CUPCAKES
It's better than saying I hope he gets electrocuted, isn't it?

LONGSHOE
Go back to clown's college.

ICE
I told you dudes about letting him see too much TV. The boob-tube gives cancer of the eyeball—but in your case—

OMAR
Weak—weak boo-boo.
(*All join in booing* ICE)

CUPCAKES
Holy dingleberries, Batman—your shit stinks too.

JUAN
O.K., everybody, let give them something for effort—two ha-ha's for Ice and one tee-hee for Cakes . . . Ready . . . tee-hee, ha-ha.
(NETT *appears outside gate*)

NETT
On the gate.
(NETT *enters*)

JUAN
. . . And one boo for Mr. Nett.

ALL

Boo . . .

CUPCAKES

Fuck this, I'm going to take a shower.
(CUPCAKES *goes into shower*)

MR. NETT

(*To* JUAN)
Poet, you've got a visit.

JUAN

'Bout time—I know Mamy ain't gonna let me swim this
ocean by my lonesome—

MR. NETT

You too, Murphy—

JUAN

Come on, let's not keep the people waiting.

LONGSHOE

I refuse my visit, Mr. Nett.

MR. NETT

That's up to you.

JUAN

You what? Man, what kinda talk is that about—your people hustled out here from the Island and you refuse? You
gonna show like Cagney?

LONGSHOE

Juan, I like you, but don't go in my kitchen without my
permission.

JUAN
Solid on that . . . later . . .
(*Enter* BROWN)

BROWN
All right, listen up. Anyone for religious services?

EL RAHEEM
Yeah, I'm going, Mr. Brown.
(*Various ad-libs*)

OMAR
How about some pussy?

BROWN
You better watch your mouth, punk, or I'll put my foot up your ass.
(*Exit* BROWN *and* EL RAHEEM)

LONGSHOE
Juan—wait . . . it's cool, man . . .

JUAN
Sure—sure, man—it's cool. Me and you's all right . . .

LONGSHOE
Juan—wait, don't make your visit—don't go, man . . .

JUAN
What? Not to make my visit . . . You must be out of your mind, Shoes . . .

LONGSHOE
Don't, man . . . The freak . . . He's gonna . . . man,

like I feel it . . . You gonna seem out of place when you show back—it's gonna be like when you step out of the joint . . . The impact . . . Everything's coming down . . . and bang, knocks you dead on your ass . . . And you fight to get up . . . And all you can do is throw a brick . . . cause that's the only thing that carries any weight . . . Dig where that's at, Juan . . . You in the life . . . you know.

JUAN

Only thing I know is that you been fucking with them A trains, again.

OMAR

Yeah, and that goddamn homemade wine.

LONGSHOE

That's right . . . But you know like everyone else knows that I know what I'm saying even if I don't say it out loud . . .

MR. NETT

Murphy, you're lucky I don't lock you up for being stoned.

LONGSHOE

You wouldn't do that, Mr. Nett. Mr. Nett . . . You wouldn't do that, Mr. Nett . . . What would happen to your bread on the white side of the road.

PACO

Hey man, be cool, Shoe.

LONGSHOE

I said white side, Paco, not Puerto Rican . . .

MR. NETT

Murphy . . .

LONGSHOE

I should have you call me *Mister* Murphy . . . *Mister* Nett . . .

MR. NETT

Don't push it, Murphy.

PACO

If I blow . . . you gonna answer.

MR. NETT

Listen, Murphy, if you don't want your visit, that all right with me . . . I give less than a fuck . . . That's your right . . . Coming, Juan?

LONGSHOE

No.

JUAN

Don't do that . . . Don't ever do that again . . . Don't ever attempt to think for me. I don't know where your head's at . . . But I can't see what the freak has to do with . . .

NETT

(*Crossing to shower*)
Mercado.

LONGSHOE

Man, he has everything to do with it . . . Don't you see he has the mark on . . . Like I said before, it's the same thing as coming out of the joint . . . You're branded . . . A week . . . a month . . . sooner or later they're gonna take you off the count . . . You know that . . . What makes you think his place is any different . . . It's all the same thing . . .

JUAN

You lost me, but keep me lost . . . cause I gotta feeling I ain't gonna like it if you find me . . .

LONGSHOE

Go on, get your part of it . . . But don't bring it back on the floor cause if you do you better walk pretty hard, Juan . . .

JUAN

No, Shoes . . . I walk soft but I hits hard . . . Dig this . . . visits and mail . . . that's my ounce of freedom and I ain't gonna give it up for nobody.
(NETT *and* JUAN *exit, gate closes.*
   LONGSHOE *gets sick and vomits into toilet, upstage center.*
   ICE *and* OMAR *cross upstage to* LONGSHOE)

ICE

You better get Mr. Nett.

OMAR

Hey, Mr. Nett. You better come in here, Shoe is sick.
(NETT *appears outside gate*)

NETT

On the gate.
(*Gate opens,* NETT *enters.*
   OMAR, ICE, *and* NETT *help* LONGSHOE *to gate, exit. Gate closes.*

PACO *alone in room, with* CUPCAKES *in shower.* PACO *flushes toilet and waits until men have crossed catwalk above. He enters shower and joins* CUPCAKES *singing.* PACO *sneaks up on* CUPCAKES *and embraces and kisses him on the neck)*

CUPCAKES

What the fuck . . . Hey, git the fuck off me, motherfucker . . . Paco . . . man, what's the matter with you . . .

PACO

Matter? What's the matter with you?

CUPCAKES

You know what's the matter with me, man . . . I don't play that shit, man.

PACO

Don't play what?

CUPCAKES

You know what . . . Don't push me, man.

PACO

Don't play what?

CUPCAKES

That faggot shit.

PACO

Man, cause I kiss you doesn't mean you're a faggot.

CUPCAKES

It means you're a faggot . . . Don't do it again.

PACO

And if I do, what you gonna do.

CUPCAKES

Nothing . . . I ain't saying I'm gonna do anything . . .

PACO

Then why should I stop . . . I dig it . . .

CUPCAKES

I don't . . . And I'm telling you to stop and don't . . .

PACO

You're telling me? Boy, you don't tell me nothing.

CUPCAKES

Stop pushing on me . . . Look, I'm asking you . . .

PACO

Go on and ask me . . . Ask me like a daddy should be asked . . .

CUPCAKES

You're treading on me, man.

PACO

¿Y qué? Oyeme, negrito . . . déjame decirte algo . . . Tú me tiene loco . . . me desespera . . . Nene, estoy en-chulao contigo . . . Yo quiero ser tuyo y quiero que tú sea mio . . . ¿Y qué tu quiere que yo haga por tí?

CUPCAKES

Que me deje quieto . . . Yo no soy un maricón . . .

PACO

Papisito, yo no estoy diciendo que tú ere maricon . . . Yo
no pienso así . . .

CUPCAKES

¿Y que tú piensa?

PACO

Que te quiero y que te adoro . . . nene.

CUPCAKES

No soy nene . . .

PACO

Tú va a ser mio . . . mi nene lindo . . . Cupcakes, que
dio bendiga la tierra que tú pise . . .

CUPCAKES

Hecha, que está caliente, Paco.

PACO

Pue ponme frio.

CUPCAKES

Paco, por favor, déjame ya. Cabrón.

PACO

Hijo la gran puta . . . punk, I ought to take you now.

CUPCAKES

Leave me alone . . . déjame.

PACO

Listen, little brother . . . I don't want nothing from you
the hard way.

CUPCAKES

Well, that's all you gonna get out of me, a hard way to go
. . . and don't you ever call me brother . . . If you considered me your brother, would you be trying this shit . . .

PACO

Si mi hermano era tan lindo como tú . . . yeah . . .

CUPCAKES

You're sick . . .

PACO

I'm what? Sick—don't you say that to me . . . Sick . . .
Shit, I'm sick cause I'm in love with you . . .

CUPCAKES

Love me . . . You use words that you don't even know the
meaning of. Brother . . . Love . . . Shit, there's a gringo
. . . who does it to little girls . . . and you wanna mess
with me . . . Why don't you hit on him . . . why? Cause
he's white . . . and you scared of the Whitey . . . But
you'll fuck over your own kind . . . He's the one you
should be cracking on . . . He's the one. Not me . . . But
you're scared of him . . .

PACO

I fear nobody . . . or anything, man . . . God or spirits.
Beside . . . I don't want him, I want you . . .

CUPCAKES

But you can't have me.

PACO

Push comes to shove, I'll take you. But I don't wanna do

that cause I know I'm gonna have to hurt you in the doing.
Look, man, I'll go both ways with you. Who you looking
for? Juan is on the visit. And let me tell you this. Makes me
no difference if he does have your back.
(BROWN *appears outside gate*)

BROWN
On the gate.
(*Gate opens.* OMAR *enters.* BROWN *exits. Gate closes*)

PACO
I'm going to have you . . . if I want you . . . right now
. . . I'm gonna show you I ain't scared of nobody . . .
cause you need to know that you gota man protecting
you . . . I'm gonna take that honky and you're gonna
help.

OMAR
What?

PACO
(*Crossing to gate*)
Hey, hey, officer, officer.
(BROWN *reappears at the gate*)

BROWN
On the gate.
(BROWN *opens gate,* PACO *exits, gate closes,* BROWN *exits*)

OMAR
Why you let that creep talk to you that way . . . All you
gotta do is swing and keep swinging. Fuck it if you lose.
Fuck it if you win. Makes no change either way. Just let

him know you's a man. I ain't the smartest guy in the world . . . but I do know that some people you can talk to, some people you gotta fight.

CUPCAKES
I took a swing at him.

OMAR
Not hard enough . . . Not at the right place. You should wait till Juan is here.

CUPCAKES
I don't wanna use Juan.

OMAR
Bullshit. If you're drowning, you use anything. You's a fine motherfucker, Cupcakes. Like I said, I ain't the smartest guy in the place. But I get the feeling you like being a fine motherfucker. And maybe . . .

CUPCAKES
Look, look . . . we're gonna do it to the white freak.

OMAR
I'm down . . . either way.

CUPCAKES
What you mean, either way.

OMAR
I like you, Cupcakes. But if you're gonna give it up . . . with an excuse . . . I want some.
(*Crossing above on catwalk, left to right, are* LONGSHOE *and* ICE)

LONGSHOE

Yeah . . . man, let me tell you, Ice, that old man put up one hell of a fight. He was about sixty years old. But he was hard as nails. Later in court I found out he was a merchant seaman.

(*Exit above,* LONGSHOE *and* ICE. BROWN *and* EL RAHEEM *appear at gate*)

BROWN

On the gate.

(BROWN *opens gate*)

EL RAHEEM

(*Ad-libs ending with*)

Why don't you come on down to religious services some-time?

BROWN

No, I was born a Christian and I'll die a Christian.

(BROWN *leaves room, letting* LONGSHOE *and* ICE *enter, closes gate and exits*)

ICE

You think you got it beat.

LONGSHOE

Oh yeah, no doubt about it . . . Like when we went to court . . . He told the judge that I was Spanish . . . and that I spoke it when I was ripping him off. Cause the old man is South American. I told the judge I could hardly speak English, let alone some mira-mira language. The Legal Aid said we got one good chance behind that.

(PACO's *voice comes from offstage right. Ad-libs about drag queens that have just been arrested.*

BROWN *and* PACO *appear at gate*)

BROWN

On the gate.

(*Enter* PACO)

OMAR

Hey, look, some fags . . . They bringing in some drag queens on the floor . . . Oy, baby . . . hey, sweet mama . . . Over here, check this out . . . ten inches.

(ICE *joins* OMAR *to make some remarks to the "girls," or drag queens, offstage*)

ICE

Fuck that, check this out . . . Thirteen inches.

(*Enter* JUAN)

JUAN

That belongs to Paco. Hey, what's happening, Ice . . . don't tell me you are into that scene.

(BROWN *closes gate and exits*)

ICE

Juan . . . a stiff dick knows no conscience . . . How was the visit?

JUAN

Beautiful . . . Told her to chalk the bail money up . . . just go for the lawyer. I think that's more important . . . don't you?

ICE

Yeah, it is . . . if I had somebody out there looking out for me, I'd do the same thing . . .

JUAN

She's not very pretty . . . not very bright . . . but she's all I have, man, and I burn her every night.

ICE

Damn, Juan, speaking of burning somebody, did I ever tell you about the first time I was upstate?—Clinton, to be exact.

OMAR

Yeah, I heard it before. The old Jane Fonda shit.

ICE

Well, Juan ain't heard it.

OMAR

Tell it to Juan.

JUAN

Go on, run it.

ICE

You know how hard it was to get short heist up in big-foot country before the riot.

LONGSHOE

What you mean before the riot—it still hard to cop short heist up there. People still making money renting the damn things out.

OMAR

Yeah, but it was harder then. Now they don't really give that much attention to short heist. Like before, they would keep-lock you. Now they just take them away.

JUAN

When I was in Cax—it was terrible up there. Man, I still hear tell they got the old track system running.

CUPCAKES

What's the track system?

JUAN

Segregation between inmates . . . Like black and white handball courts . . . water fountains, you know like . . .

ICE

If you're white you can't smoke after a black. Sit at the same table in the messhall, and if you do you can't eat your food. No taking anything from a black person. Like if you're a Whitey and you playing handball and your ball goes over on the black handball court and a black touches it, well you and the black have to fight. If you don't, you go on the track and become a creep.

CUPCAKES

Break it down.

ICE

Break it down, Juan.

JUAN

For instance, the yard is broken down in three sections.

ICE

Four. The track makes four.

JUAN

Yah, you're right. One white, one black, one Spanish-speaking.

ICE

Ricans, baby, Ricans.

PACO

Yah, there was Cubans up there.

JUAN

. . . 'n Mexicans 'n Dominicans 'n South Americans.

ICE

Same damn thing. They all eat rice 'n beans.

JUAN

You gotta lotta shit with you, Ice. But you're right. The track makes four. And if you're considered good people, you stay with your people and enjoy their protection. If you ain't good people and—like—go against the program your people set up . . .

ICE

Convicts' law of survival. The codes of crime.

JUAN

Well, anyway, you go to the track with the creeps . . . with no protection but your own two hands . . . dig.

ICE

Man, fuck that, he'll learn when he gets there . . . Dig this . . . I was in my cell . . . like this is where they have all those French Canadian bigots. Let me tell you I was raised in Georgia for a while, but like I swear to God I never seen anybody as racist as a French Canadian. Anyway, like I was in my cell about nine, dig. I was reading this short-heist book. Brother man, this was a smoker. S . . . M . . . O . . . K . . . E . . . R. Just after a few pages . . . I had to put down the damn book because my Johnson Ronson was ripping through my cheap underwears. So I put the book down . . . jumped out my bed . . . stick the mirrors out the cell . . . to see if anybody was coming down the gallery . . . Coast clear . . . Like upstate you know ain't like down here. You ain't got no cellies, Cupcakes . . . you be by yourself. So I would really stretch out in doing up my wood . . . I got this picture of Jane Fonda. Cause you can't have nothing on the walls. She's got this black silk satin bikini. Man, I could almost touch those fine white tits of hers. And that cute round butt sticking out and all. Dig. I strip naked . . . and started rolling. She was looking good on my mind.

OMAR
Why a white girl?

ICE
Cause, sucker, we weren't allow to have short-heist pictures . . . and how many black girls have taken short-heist flicks.

JUAN
Hundreds of them. And hundreds of Puerto Rican girls too.

ICE
Yeah, well . . . I guess I wanted a white girl.

EL RAHEEM
You wanted a girl so bad . . . made him no different if it was just imagination.

ICE
Hey, man, you guys gonna let me tell this thing or what?

OMAR

Ain't nobody stopping you. Run it. Juan's listenin'.

ICE

Yeah, she was sure looking good on my mind . . . Jesus
. . . So I started calling out her name real softly . . . Jane
. . . Jane . . . Janeeee . . . oooo Janeee baby. Ooooo
Janneeee baby . . .
(LONGSHOE *shows short-heist book to* ICE. *Inmates gather around table*)

OMAR

Goddamn! Will you look at the gash on that girl. That's
pure polyunsaturated pussy.

ICE

Wesson Oil never had it so good. Oh, Jane baby. Oh Jane
mama. Ooooo Jane. Come here, get a part of some reallll
downnnn home gut-stomped black buck fucking . . . Man,
I was really running. Wow. She was in front of me. Dancing, spreading her legs wider and wider . . . Till I could
see her throatmmm. Them white thighs crushing me to
death. Wiggling and crawling on the floor. Calling her
name out, Janneee babyyyyy . . . ooooo Janeeee baby
. . . This is black power. Git honey, git honey, git git git
. . . ununhahahaha . . . mmmmm, calling her name out
faster, a little bit louder. A little bit faster, a little bit
louder . . . And I'm whipping my Johnson to the bone
. . . Soon everybody on the tier knew I was working out
cause soon everybody's voices is with me. And we're all
tryin' to get this one last big nut together. . . . Git it, git
it. Janneeee . . . baby . . . Get it, get it, get it, get it, get
it, get it, get it. I scream, my knees buckle . . . and I'm
kneeling there, beat as a son of a bitch, because that's the

way I felt, beat as a son of a bitch. I really burnt Jane that
night. You know if I ever meet that broad, Jane Fonda . . .
(BROWN *and* CLARK *appear at gate*)

BROWN
On the gate . . .
(CLARK *enters,* BROWN *closes gate,* BROWN *exits*)

ICE
I'm going to ask her if she ever felt a strange sensation
that night. Anyway, brother man . . . I turn my head and
bang.
(CLARK *walks over to* JUAN)

CLARK
Can I see you, please. I need to talk to you, please.

JUAN
Later.

CLARK
Please.

ICE
The man said later. You're interrupting me . . . creep.

PACO
Go to your place, maricón. You know . . . go on, man,
bang, then what happened.

ICE
Oh yeah, bang. I happened to look up and there's these
two redneck . . . peckerwood big-foot country honkies
. . . looking and grinning at me . . . I don't know how

they was there cause I had my eyes close all the time I was
gitting my rocks off, better for the imagination. Helps the
concentration, dig. They weren't saying a word, just standing there grinning . . . grinning these two big grins . . .
these two real big grins on the faces that reach from one ear
to the other. So I started grinning back. Grinning th—that
old nigger grin we give to Charlie . . . We stood there
grinning at each other for about five minutes . . . them
grinning at my Johnson . . . me grinning at them grinning at my Johnson . . . just grinning . . . Hold it, no
really, just grinning. It's weird. Freaky kinda thing.
Somebody stops to watch you masturbate, then stands there
grinning at you. I mean like what can you say. Really, what
can you say to them. To anybody. All of a sudden the
biggest one with the biggest grin gives out a groan. "Hey,
Harry, this fucking face has been pulling his pecker on a
white woman." So Harry comes over and said very intel-
ligently, "Da . . . da . . . this ain't no white woman, Joey.
I mean, no real white woman. She's a Communist, Joey, she
really is, da . . . da . . . she's white trash, Joey. Take my
word for it, she's white trash. The *Daily News* said so." So
Joey runs this down on Harry: "Harry, I know what she is
. . . I read the papers, too, you know. But she is a white
woman. And this nigger has been thinking about . . . having screwed her. Now you know that's un-American. Harry,
open up the dead lock." So Harry runs to open up the dead
lock. Now Joey got the nigger knocker wrapped around his
hand real tight, dig. I know he about to correct me on some
honky rules. I know what's about to jump off . . . I'm in
my cell . . . And I'm cool . . . extra cool . . . That's my
name . . . Ice . . . The lames roll in front of my cell and
I go into my Antarctic frigid position . . . you can see the
frost all over my cell. But before Harry could open the dead
lock . . . I told him, Joey baby . . . now, I'm locking up

on the third tier . . . I said, Joey baby . . . I sure hope
you can fly. He said, What you talking about, nigger boy.
I said fly like a bird. You know F-L-Y. Cause once you open
this gate . . . I ain't about to let you whip me with that
stick. I stood up on my toes. Pointed over the rail and said
both of us are going, Joey. He yelled out, Harry, don't up
the gate. This nigger crazy. Now I'm a crazy nigger cause I
wouldn't let them come in here and kick me in my ass.

CUPCAKES
So what happened after that?

ICE
What happen, they called in reinforcement and tear-gassed
me out the cell.

CUPCAKES
Tear-gas you in the cell?

ICE
Yeah, what you think they do, ask you pretty please, would
you come out of your cell, we would like to break open
your skull.

JUAN
Ain't nothing new about that . . . Happens all the time.

ICE
Anyway, when I comes out the hospital, I had to go see the
psych . . .

CUPCAKES
For what.

ICE

For masturbating. And for not letting them crack my head willingly. You see only crazy people beat their meat.

CUPCAKES

I must be a lunatic.

PACO

The only lunatic is the freak.
(NETT *appears at gate*)

NETT

On the gate.
(*Opens gate*)
Sick call. Line up for sick call.

PACO

Come, I hear they got a brand-new nurse on.
(EXIT LONGSHOE, PACO, CUPCAKES *with various ad-libs*)

OMAR

Now what you got, the leg? Or is it the tooth?

ICE

Look, Jack, you had the leg last week.

OMAR

Fuck that, I'll take the tooth.
(*Exit* OMAR *and* ICE.
   NETT *closes gate on* EL RAHEEM *and exits*)

EL RAHEEM

Mr. Brown, Mr. Brown—I want to go to sick call.
(BROWN *appears outside gate*)

BROWN
On the gate.
(BROWN *opens gate, lets* EL RAHEEM *out, closes gate, and both exit.* CLARK *and* JUAN *are left alone on stage*)

JUAN
What you want to see me about, Clark?

CLARK
Look, what I told you earlier . . . er . . . that between me and you . . . like, I don't know why I even said that, just . . . just that . . . man, like everything was just coming down on me . . . My wife . . . she was at the hospital . . . She . . . she didn't even look at me . . . once, not once . . . Please . . . don't let it out . . . please . . . I'll really go for help this time . . . I promise.

JUAN
What happened at the P.I. stand?

CLARK
Nothing . . . nothing . . . happened . . .

JUAN
Did she identify you? Did she?

CLARK
I don't know. I didn't see anybody. They put me next to a bunch of the other men about my size, weight . . . You—the whole line-up routine. I didn't see anybody or anything but the people there and this voice that kept asking me to turn around to say, "Hello, little girl." That's all.

JUAN
Nothing else?

CLARK

No.

JUAN

You mean they didn't make you sign some papers?

CLARK

No.

JUAN

Was there a lawyer for you there? Somebody from the courts?

CLARK

Juan, I really don't know . . . I didn't see anybody . . . and they didn't let me speak to anyone at all . . . They hustled me in and hustled me right out . . .

JUAN

That means you have a chance to beat this case . . . Did they tell you what they are holding you for?

CLARK

No . . . no one told me anything.

JUAN

If they are rushing it—the P.I.—that could mean they only are waiting on the limitation to run out.

CLARK

What does that all mean?

JUAN

What it means is that you will get a chance to scar up some more little girls' minds.

CLARK

Don't say that, Juan. Please don't think like that. Believe me, if I thought I couldn't seek help after this ordeal, I would have never—I mean, I couldn't do that again.

JUAN

How many times you've said that in the street and wind up molesting some kid in the park.

CLARK

Believe me, Juan . . . please believe me. I wouldn't any more.

JUAN

Why should I?

CLARK

Cause I told you the truth before. I told you what I haven't told God.

JUAN

That's because God isn't in the House of Detention.

CLARK

Please, Juan, why are you being this way? What have I done to you?

JUAN

What have you done to me? What you've done to me? It's what you've done, period. It's the stand that you are forcing me to take.

CLARK

You hate me.

JUAN

I don't hate you. I hate what you've done. What you are capable of doing. What you might do again.

CLARK

You sound like a judge.

JUAN

In this time and place I am your judge.

CLARK

No . . . no. You are not . . . And I'm sick and tired of people judging me.

JUAN

Man, I don't give a fuck what you're sick and tired about. What you told about yourself was done because of the pressure. People say and do weird things under pressure.

CLARK

I'm not used to this.

JUAN

I don't care what you're used to. I got to make some kind of thing about you.

CLARK

No, you don't have to do anything. Just let me live.

JUAN

Let you live?

CLARK

I can't make this . . . this kind of life. I'll die.

JUAN

Motherfucker, don't cry on me.

CLARK

Cry . . . why shouldn't I cry . . . why shouldn't I feel sorry for myself . . . I have a right to . . . I have some rights . . . and when these guys get back from the sick call . . . I'm gonna tell them what the captain said to me, that if anybody bothers me to tell him . . .

JUAN

Then you will die.

CLARK

I don't care one way or the other. Juan, when I came here I already had been abused by the police . . . threatened by a mob the newspaper created . . . Then the judge, for my benefit and the benefit of society, had me committed to observation. Placed in an isolated section of some nut ward . . . viewed by interns and visitors like some abstract object, treated like a goddamn animal monster by a bunch of inhuman, incompetent, third-rate, unqualified, unfit psychopaths calling themselves doctors.

JUAN

I know the scene.

CLARK

No, you don't know . . . electros—sedatives—hypnosis—therapy . . . humiliated by some crank nurses who strapped me to my bed and played with my penis to see if it would get hard for "big girls like us."

JUAN

Did it?

CLARK

Yeah . . . yes, it did.

JUAN

My father used to say he would fuck 'em from eight to eighty, blind, cripple, and/or crazy.

CLARK

Juan, you are the only human being I've met.

JUAN

Don't try to leap me up . . . cause I don't know how much of a human being I would be if I let you make the sidewalk. But there's no way I could stop you short of taking you off the count.
(NETT *appears at gate*)

NETT

On the gate.
(NETT *opens gate. The rest of the men enter.* NETT *closes gate and exits*)

ICE

Juan . . . come here for a second.

JUAN

Yeah, what is it, Ice?

ICE

Juan, if you remember what was said after the last riot here.

PACO

He should. He suggested it, didn't he?

JUAN

I remember everything that was said.

ICE

Anything that would affect the whole floor . . . we would hold council on it, right? Well, he affects the whole floor.

JUAN

What's happening?

LONGSHOE

He white like I am . . . And you ain't got no right according to the rules to take his back . . . if he is stuff.

JUAN

Stuff? He ain't stuff.

LONGSHOE

Well, we say he is.

JUAN

Who says he is?

ALL

I say he is.

PACO

Anybody that has to rape little girls is a faggot. He's stuff . . . squeeze.

JUAN

I say he ain't.

ICE

You got no say in this.

PACO

Oh, he's got a say, not that it means anything, but he's got a say.

LONGSHOE

Paco, be cool.

JUAN

Yeah, Paco, be very cool.

LONGSHOE

That ain't necessary. And neither is your getting in the way of the council.

JUAN

The council was set up to help, not to destroy.

PACO

The council was set up to help, not to destroy. Oh, would you listen to this . . . Very . . . very pretty . . . He's fucking Cupcakes and now he's fucking the white freak.

CUPCAKES

Ain't nobody fucking me, Paco.

PACO

Maybe he's not yet, but he's setting you up. Giving you fatherly advice, my ass. He's just like El Raheem. He wants to fuck you too. Putting the wisdom in front of the knowledge. He's calling you a girl. That's what he means by that. And Omar playing exercises with you so that you can take showers together. Longshoe . . . giving you short-heist books. Everybody wants you, Cupcakes. Cupcakes, Ice gave you that name, didn't he? Wasn't that your woman's name in the street, Ice? . . . Nobody saying anything.

Why? Cause I hit the truth. Pushed that little button . . . Everybody on the whole floor is trying to cop . . . but only Juan gets a share. Now he wants the white freak for himself, too.

JUAN
You're sick, man.

PACO
Tu madre . . . tu madre, maricón . . . hijo de la gran puta . . . cabrón.
(PACO *lunges toward* JUAN)

ICE
Hold it . . . hold it . . . Man, why fight each other over some bullshit.

JUAN
Let the motherfucker go. Let him go.

PACO
All right . . . all right, let me go. I'll be cool. O.K., Juan. Check this out. I want him. Longshoe is white. He gave the O.K. That means he wants him. Omar getting a share. So does El Raheem.

JUAN
El Raheem, you are in this too?

EL RAHEEM
He's a Whitey. A devil. Anything goes.

PACO
How about you, Cupcakes?

JUAN

Julio?

PACO

Well, it's either him or . . . well, Cakes . . . make up
your choice, now. Which way? Who you stand with?

CUPCAKES

I go . . . I go with you.

JUAN

You punk, you little punk. Everything I taught you just
went in one ear and came out the other. You want to be an
animal too . . . You're letting this place destroy you.

PACO

Ice, which way?

ICE

Man, I . . . I don't want no part of it.

PACO

You what? You want no part of it?

ICE

You heard what I said. Juan is right. This place makes animals out of us.

PACO

Man.

ICE

Man what? You think anybody here is good enough to
take me.

JUAN
Take us.

PACO
That's the way you want it.

ICE
That the way it is.

EL RAHEEM
Ice, you don't have to take whole part.

OMAR
Ice, you my man . . . but you sticking up for some honky
is wrong . . . You going upstate, you know that. Juan is
likely to hit the street. He got somebody out there. You
don't. All you got is a plea to cop. I dig you a whole lot.
But you're wrong, Ice.

LONGSHOE
You don't have to take part, play chickie . . . that's all
. . . play chickie . . .

ICE
I . . . I . . . all right . . . I'll play chickie . . .

JUAN
You still got me to deal with . . .
(PACO *grabs* JUAN *from behind*)

PACO
Hold him, Ice.
(ICE *holds* JUAN)

JUAN
Let me go, Ice. Ice, don't do this to yourself. Ice, let me go.

CLARK

Mr. Nett. Mr. Nett . . .
(CLARK *runs to window ledge upstage center.* OMAR *jumps on ledge with him.*

NETT *appears at gate, opens it, walks in, sees what's happening, and turns to go, but remains*)
O.K. O.K. Don't hurt me any more. Go 'head, do what you want. Go 'head, you filthy bastards. Go 'head, Mr. Nett, don't think you can walk away from this. I'll tell the captain. I'll bring you all before the courts. You bastards. You too, you fat faggot.

JUAN

Shut up . . . shut up.

PACO

You gonna do what?
(PACO *pulls out homemade knife*)

LONGSHOE

He's gonna squeal. He's gonna rat us out.
(OMAR *jumps off window ledge*)

JUAN

Ice, let him go.

EL RAHEEM

You're in this too, Ice. We'll all get more time.

CLARK

I'll make sure you get life, you son of a bitch.

MR. NETT

I'll lose my job.
(*Opens gate to look down corridor*)

CLARK

I'll make sure you go to jail. My father has money . . . plenty money.

JUAN

Shut up, Clark . . . shut up.
(PACO *runs toward* CLARK *to kill him.* EL RAHEEM *restrains him*)

PACO

I ain't doing no more time than I have to.

OMAR

Paco, that murder.

CUPCAKES

What are we going to do?

LONGSHOE

Kill the motherfucking rat.

MR. NETT

Kill him—it's self-defense.

EL RAHEEM

Suicide . . . suicide . . . He did it to himself.

JUAN

It's murder. Ice, it's murder. You'll be a part of it, too.

PACO

Hold him, Ice.

CUPCAKES

I don't want to do more time.

LONGSHOE

Kill him . . . kill him . . . kill the sick motherfucker.
(LONGSHOE *pulls* CLARK *off window ledge*)

PACO

Here, El . . . He's a devil . . . kill him . . . You said
the devil is gonna die anyway.
(PACO *gives the knife to* EL RAHEEM)

OMAR

Kill him, El . . . kill him.

EL RAHEEM

Hold him . . . hold him . . .
(CLARK *runs to downstage right corner.* OMAR *and* LONG-
SHOE *grab him and hold him*)

PACO

Stab him.

MR. NETT

No, cut his throat.

EL RAHEEM

Cut his throat.

PACO

Do it, El . . . Do it, El.
(EL *brings the knife down to* CLARK's *neck*)

LONGSHOE

Go on, nigger, kill him.

EL RAHEEM

I can't . . . I can't . . . I don't have the heart . . . I
can't . . . do it.

LONGSHOE

What you mean? You can do it . . . You talk of killing Whitey every day.

EL RAHEEM

I can't do it. I just can't kill a man like that. Not that way. Get up and fight, honky. Let him up and I could do it.

LONGSHOE

Kill him . . . standing up . . . laying down . . . sitting . . . Either way, he's dead.

EL RAHEEM

It's not the same thing . . . I just can't do it.

LONGSHOE

Kill him . . . kill him.

PACO

He's a devil, El Raheem.

CUPCAKES

Oh, my God.
(CUPCAKES *pushes* EL RAHEEM *to shower and restrains him*)

JUAN

Don't, El, don't do it. That's not the way a black god kills. That's a devil's way.

CLARK

Please . . . don't kill me . . please, I didn't mean what I said. I didn't mean it. I won't tell anybody . . . please do what you want but don't kill me. I got a wife and kids. Please don't . . . please.

EL RAHEEM
(*Breaking loose from* CUPCAKES, *tries once more to kill* CLARK)
Allah Akbar, Allah Akbar, I can't do it—I just can't do it.

LONGSHOE
Give that knife, punk.
(*Swings knife, cutting* CLARK'S *throat*)
Scream, bastard . . . rat . . . Scream . . . monster . . . die . . . die . . .
(*Everyone is silent.*
      NETT *closes gate and exits*)

OMAR
El Raheem . . . black god . . . leader of the black nation . . . faggot . . .

EL RAHEEM
I'm not a faggot . . . I'm not a punk . . . Omar, believe me. It's just that I couldn't kill a man looking at me helpless.

LONGSHOE
You punk motherfucker you . . . You ain't nothing but a jiveass nigger. I'm gonna cut your black ass until you turn white, nigger.

CUPCAKES
El . . .

ICE
Shoe . . . raise . . . or deal with me.

LONGSHOE

You want a part of this, too, Ice? . . . Nigger, you want a part of this?

ICE

Don't run it in the hole, Shoe.

LONGSHOE

You selling me a ticket, faggot?

ICE

That's right, honky. You feel you can cash it?

LONGSHOE

Come with it.

ICE

You bring it and bring your best.

(LONGSHOE *rushes* ICE, *swings the knife.* ICE *jumps out of the way.* PACO *throws chair to* ICE)

LONGSHOE

Come, nigger. What's the matter, jig. You can't stand the sight of a knife. You bought this . . . now enjoy it. Come baby, don't run.

PACO

Ice.

LONGSHOE

Paco, you go against me?

ICE

Come, punk, now he stand on equal grounds.

LONGSHOE
You'll only get one shot, faggot.

ICE
That's all I need.

PACO
Don't look at me, Longshoe. You wanna kill each other, then go ahead. El que gane pierde.

LONGSHOE
Whoever wins loses.

ICE
Dirty cocksucker. Fuck it.

CUPCAKES
Stop it, goddamn it. Stop it . . . Oh, my God . . . is this really us.

BLACKOUT

EPILOGUE

That evening. In dim light, NETT *searches dayroom for remaining evidence, which he puts in shower. Closes shower curtain. Meanwhile, roll call is in progress.* BROWN *is on catwalk. As he calls out names, prisoners appear in their respective positions on the catwalk above.*

BROWN
All right, listen up . . . When I call out your name . . . give me your cell location and your first name . . . Come out of your cell . . . Leave everything behind . . . Keep your mouth shut . . . eyes front . . . hands over your head. Blinker.

OMAR
Omar, upper D 9.

BROWN
Johnson.

JOHNSON
El Raheem, William, lower D 4.

BROWN
Pasqual.

PACO
Paco Pasqual, lower D 2.

BROWN
Wicker.

ICE
John, lower D 5.

BROWN
Murphy.

LONGSHOE
Charles, lower D 7.

BROWN
Otero.

JUAN
Juan, upper D 3.

BROWN
Mercado.

CUPCAKES
Julio, upper D 2.

BROWN
Put on your clothes and report to the dayroom . . .
(NETT *remains. Enter* ALLARD)

ALLARD
Get the lights on in here.

NETT

On the lights.
(*Lights on in dayroom*)

ALLARD

Get Merkaydo and Murphy.

NETT

Mercado, Murphy, in the dayroom.

BROWN

Mercado and Murphy.
(CUPCAKES *and* LONGSHOE *leave cells offstage and cross cat-walk, left to right, led by* BROWN. *They appear at entrance to dayroom*)

BROWN

Which one first?

NETT

Mercado.
(CUPCAKES *and* BROWN *enter dayroom and* BROWN *searches* CUPCAKES. BROWN *leaves dayroom, closes gate, but remains outside it*)

ALLARD

Merkaydo, possession of drugs and sale of drugs.

CUPCAKES

Mi nombre es Mercado. Yo no hablo inglés.

ALLARD

You no what. Listen here, you little punk. I don't hear this speaka la english jazz. I'm not here to play games with you. That's why we give you recreation. The only game I'm going to play with you is to break your little Puerto Rican ass and slam you in the bing until you leave this place. Is this clear? Now you speak English, don't you?

CUPCAKES

Yes, sir, perfeckly.

ALLARD

Now, that's sales and possession of drugs, right?

CUPCAKES

Like, man . . . Marijuana ain't no drug.

ALLARD

(*Almost shouting*)

My name is Captain Allard, my name is not man . . . Do you understand that? Well, say so.

CUPCAKES

Yes, sir.

ALLARD

O.K. Let's see, your name is Merkaydo.

CUPCAKES

Mercado.

ALLARD

Jewleo.

CUPCAKES

Julio.

ALLARD

You are twenty-one years old and here for selling drugs. I wonder how many school kids you got hooked on this stuff.

CUPCAKES

I hooked no one onto anything, man.

ALLARD

What did you say?

CUPCAKES

I mean, sir.

ALLARD

You were in the dayroom when this happened, weren't you?

CUPCAKES

Yes, sir, he borrowed my towel, sir.

ALLARD

He borrowed your towel, went into the shower, and cut his throat? Why did you lend him your towel?

CUPCAKES

To dry himself.

ALLARD

What were you doing while he was in the shower?

CUPCAKES

I was watching TV and rapping to the fellas.

ALLARD

What program were you watching?

CUPCAKES

The Dating Game.

ALLARD

Did you know what Clark Davis was here for?

CUPCAKES

No, sir, it's none of my business.

ALLARD

Did he seem depressed, uptight?

CUPCAKES

I didn't notice.

ALLARD

Merkaydo, this is your first time up on criminal charges, isn't it?

CUPCAKES

Yes, sir.

ALLARD

Come here, Merkaydo, sit down.

CUPCAKES

No, thank you, I'd rather stand. If you don't mind, Captain.

ALLARD

Well, I do mind . . . I ask you to sit down . . . I don't like looking up.

CUPCAKES

Yes, sir . . .

ALLARD

Merkaydo . . . I don't know if you are listening to any of these jailhouse lawyers. But you should take note that all the cooperation that is given to the Department is always taken into deep consideration by the courts. Why, I've known men who didn't stand a chance in a million to walk right out into the streets, all because of a letter of recommendation from the Department. And you know, of course, this is kept in the strictest of confidence. And who knows—maybe in the future, if you should ever get arrested again, it may go well with you. Now, think about this for a moment. Do you care to make a statement?

CUPCAKES

No, no statements . . .

ALLARD

All right, go back to your cell . . . Wait a minute, Merkaydo. Has anyone on this floor been hitting on you?

CUPCAKES

No, sir.

ALLARD

If anyone did approach you with a homosexual proposition, would you report it to the officer in charge, Mr. Nett?

CUPCAKES

No, sir, I'm no rat, I'm a man . . . I take care of myself . . .

ALLARD
O.K., mister . . . Get back to your cell.

BROWN
On the gate.
(BROWN *opens gate,* CUPCAKES *exits,* BROWN *closes gate.* CUPCAKES *crosses catwalk to his position above left.* BROWN *remains at entrance below, while* ALLARD *and* NETT *continue conversation*)

ALLARD
Nett, how long has he been on your floor?

NETT
A little over a month, sir.

ALLARD
And no one has tried anything with him?

NETT
Not that I know of, sir.

ALLARD
Well, one thing's for sure, men ain't what they used to be . . .

NETT
Things have changed, sir.

ALLARD
Murphy—he's been around awhile . . .

NETT
Murphy's been in and out of these places since the day one, sir.

ALLARD
Call him in.

NETT
Yes, sir. On the gate. Murphy in the dayroom.

BROWN
Put your hands down.
(BROWN *opens gate,* LONGSHOE *enters,* BROWN *closes gate.
During following dialogue,* CUPCAKES, *on catwalk above
left, and* JUAN, *on catwalk above right, carry on a conver-
sation in Spanish about the preceding interrogation*)

ALLARD
Murphy . . . alias George Reagan . . . Michael Potter
. . . Julian Berger . . . etc. . . . Drugs . . . burglary
. . . assault . . . grand larceny . . . attempted murder
. . . Now it's armed robbery, you got quite a record,
Murphy.

LONGSHOE
Yes, sir.

ALLARD
Murphy . . . stand up straight . . . get that gum out of
your mouth . . . and wipe that smirk off your face . . .
You were in the dayroom when this happen?

LONGSHOE
Sir?

ALLARD
Were you in the dayroom when this incident concerning
Clark Davis occurred. That's a very simple question, Mur-

phy . . . And all I want is a simple answer, I'll try to keep my questions from being too profound for you.

LONGSHOE
I would appreciate it, Captain.

ALLARD
Yes, I'm sure you would . . . What were you doing while Clark Davis was bleeding to death in the shower?
(*At this point* PACO, *at entrance gate, joins Spanish conversation with* JUAN *and* CUPCAKES)

LONGSHOE
I was sitting at the table reading a book and every once in a while I'd take a glance at the boob-tube.

ALLARD
At the what?

LONGSHOE
At the television, sir . . .
(*At this point,* ICE, *on catwalk above left, and* OMAR, *on catwalk above right, talk in "ism" language*)

ALLARD
Well, say so, you're no Puerto Rican just off the banana boat. You speak English. What was the name of the book you were reading and what program did you every once in a while glance at?

LONGSHOE
The book was *Father's Little Girlfriend* and the name of the program was the Dating Game.

ALLARD

And I suppose everyone else on the floor was with you watching the Dating Game?

LONGSHOE

Yah, well, except those that were in court.

ALLARD

Nett, can't you keep those men quiet?
(NETT *crosses to entrance gate.* BROWN *exits and reappears on catwalk*)

NETT

All right, pipe down.
(*The inmates stop for a moment, then* OMAR *and* ICE *continue the "ism" talk*)

ALLARD

Sit down, Murphy, have a smoke . . .

LONGSHOE

No, thank you, Captain, I have my own . . .

ALLARD

Murphy, let me ask you a question . . . just between you and me . . . what do you know about this? Something isn't right . . . I can feel it . . . I think you know what I mean . . .

BROWN

(*On catwalk above, to* ICE)
Shut up, ol' simple ass nigger.

ICE

Your mother's father is a simple ass nigger.

BROWN

What you say?

ICE

I didn't say nothing.

BROWN

(*Pulling* ICE *from catwalk above left*)

Come on out of there—shut up—shut up—I kick you in the ass, shut up, motherfucker.

(BROWN *and* ICE *cross catwalk, left to right, and appear below at entrance gate*)

LONGSHOE

What's going on, Captain?

ALLARD

Murphy, I'm concerned about you . . . a lone white man among all these Puerto Ricans and Negroes. You're not protecting these people, are you? . . . Do you realize that every offense that has been committed against a young white boy in this place has been perpetrated by the blacks and the Puerto Ricans. What do you owe these people . . . Look, you're an old-timer from the old school, I understand that . . . and I appreciate and respect your position —but we're in a different situation here . . . Murphy, I want you to make a statement to help out in this investigation.

LONGSHOE

I make no statements to anyone . . . I got nothing to say . . .

ALLARD

All right, go back to your cell. Just a moment. Murphy, what color was his hair?

LONGSHOE
I'm color-blind, sir.

ALLARD
Get out of here! I'm color-blind!

BROWN
On the gate.
(*Gate opens.* BROWN *enters, and* LONGSHOE *exits. Gate closes*)

NETT
Want me to write him up, sir?

ALLARD
Later.

NETT
You want to see anyone else, sir?

ALLARD
What for? . . . They'll all come in here with the same story about watching the Dating Game show, and they're all lying.

NETT
What makes you think they're lying, Captain?

ALLARD
What makes me think they're lying? Let me ask you. How can a man come on this floor . . . no one talk to him . . . no one notice him, no one remember a thing about him. Nett, I came here to get the facts . . . and you are not helping.

NETT

You have no right.

ALLARD

Don't raise your voice at me, Nett. I'm no inmate.

NETT

Captain, who are you investigating, these animals or a fellow officer?

ALLARD

Don't give me that fellow-officer routine, Nett. You are a disgrace to that uniform.

NETT

Captain, those gold bars don't give you the right to abuse.

ALLARD

Nett, did you send this TV repair order to the shop or not? This is your signature, isn't it? Then I can assume that the men were not watching TV, because the television was not working . . . And can I also assume that Clark Davis's death was not a suicide . . . Do you realize what you've gotten yourself into?

NETT

Captain, he was—

ALLARD

Shut up, Nett . . . His parents are downstairs in the warden's office complaining about why he wasn't placed in a special unit . . . or given more protection. What are we supposed to say to this family? . . . I don't know if I'm doing the right thing, Nett . . . but I am going to tear up this repair order. It's the only thing that'll shake up their story, and yours as well . . .

NETT

Thank you, sir.

ALLARD

There's nothing to thank me for. I didn't do this for you, Nett, but for the Department. Do we understand each other?

NETT

Yes, sir.

ALLARD

I hope so. I'm going to recommend that these men be transferred to other floors, and I suggest that you make the same recommendation. Then you keep a tight rein on this floor and don't ever get involved with the inmates again.

NETT

Yes, sir.

ALLARD

I should demand your resignation, but I won't. I want you to take a sick leave early, like tomorrow. Write the reports first, get the men into the dayroom; I want to speak to them.

NETT

Captain, he was a child rapist . . . On the gate, everyone in the dayroom.
(BROWN *opens gate.*

ICE, EL RAHEEM, PACO *enter and cross to table area.* OMAR, CUPCAKES, LONGSHOE, *and* JUAN *exit from catwalk and enter below.* NETT *stays on.* BROWN *leaves dayroom and closes gate*)

ALLARD

I'm Captain Allard, men. I'm here investigating the terrible tragedy that occurred here today . . . And I'm satisfied that it was a suicide . . . But I would like to state that I and Clark Davis's parents hold you all morally guilty . . . If you had taken some time out of your own problems to help this poor man that was placed in here because of mistaken identity . . .

EL RAHEEM

What did you say? Mistaken identity? You mean he wasn't here because they caught him . . .

ICE

El.

ALLARD

Caught him doing what?

EL RAHEEM

With drugs . . . what else do people come to jail for?

ALLARD

No, Mr. Davis was not a drug addict. In fact, he was a very well liked and respected member of his community . . . a working man with a wife and child . . . We took him down for a positive-identification line-up . . . and the person that Mr. Davis was supposed to have assaulted was not in her right mind and had already pointed out two,

maybe five other men, as the man who assaulted her . . .
Mr. Davis was an innocent victim of circumstances . . . Innocent . . . Good night, men.

ALL
Good night.

BROWN
On the gate.
(BROWN *opens gate,* ALLARD *and* NETT *exit.* BROWN *closes
gate and* BROWN *exits*)

LONGSHOE
Man, he was guilty, I know, I could tell, I could see it in
his eyes.

EL RAHEEM
Man, he was clean.

CUPCAKES
What have we done?

ICE
Ain't no use crying over it now, Cupcakes, be cool, don't
blow your cool, kid.

PACO
Juan knows.

JUAN
I know nothing, I was watching the Dating Game.

VOICE
Mercado, on the bail.

ICE

Go on, boy, your pussy for the night has just come through . . .

EL RAHEEM

Peace!

CUPCAKES

Juan, dime la verda del tipo ese, tú sabe.

JUAN

What's there to tell. You got it all under your belt, don't you?

PACO

Oye, y qué? What difference does it make? I took part? I saw him guilty. I feel nothing, mistake, it happens, eso pasa. Someday I'll be in the streets walking, minding my own business, and then boom-boom, I'll be shot down by a police, who will say it's a mistake, I accept it, as part of my destino . . . Sí, es mi destino morir en la calle como un perro . . .

LONGSHOE

That's right, what are you holding up to Juan so much for, will that bring him back?

CUPCAKES

You talk cause you did the killing.

EL RAHEEM

He talks cuz we did the killing.

CUPCAKES

I didn't take his head, I didn't swing the knife, he did.

ICE

Cupcakes, listen to me, you killed him just as much as I did.

CUPCAKES

You? You wasn't even there.

ICE

I was there . . . I was there . . . No, I didn't swing the knife . . . and neither did you, but we're guilty by not stopping it . . . We sanctioned it . . . Only Juan is free . . .

VOICE

Julio Mercado on the bail . . .

ICE

Take it light, kid, cuz you take this place with you . . .

OMAR

Cupcake, I mean Julio, do me a favor, little brother. Call this number when you get out . . . Tell her to come up to see me . . . fast . . . Say that I need her, please, little brother, it's important.

CUPCAKES

Oye, Juan, por favor, tú sabe . . .

ICE

What you want, kid? What is it? Oh shit, Juan, this kid think you're some kind of guru. Juan, if you don't tell him something, he's gonna go out there and run this thing on someone who shouldn' hear it. Can you dig it, Juan? Get his head straight . . . Juan, can you dig where I'm coming from?

LONGSHOE
Cupcake, I've killed, and I'm not afraid to do it again, do you understand that?

JUAN
Shoe, if you run some shit on that kid again, I won't be afraid to kill, either.

EL RAHEEM
Neither would I.

JUAN
I'll give you something, a cheer, one last hooray, that's yours by law . . . cuz you're leaving this place . . . and only becuz of that, I can't give you no life-style pearls . . . no cues . . . becuz you, like the rest of us . . . became a part of the walls . . . an extra bar in the gate . . . to remain a number for the rest of your life in the street world . . .

CUPCAKES
On the gate.
(BROWN *opens gate and walks away*)

JUAN
Cupcake, you went past the money and blew it . . . yah, that's right, this is cop and blow . . . and you blew it becuz you placed yourself above understanding.

VOICE
On the bail, Mercado . . . get your ass out here now.

JUAN

Oye, espera, no corra, just one thing, brother, your fear of this place stole your spirit . . . And this ain't no pawn-shop.

BLACKOUT

GLOSSARY OF SLANG

A TRAIN   Any depressant drug. They are readily available in most prisons—at a price; guards and prisoners bring them in from the outside; also, they have a way of disappearing from the shelves of prison clinics and pharmacies.

BACK   As in "watch your back," meaning someone may attack you (usually with a knife) when you aren't looking. Prisoners attack each other from the front ("fronting") when they have some respect for their adversaries or when the attack constitutes some kind of showdown. Stabbing someone in the back is either an act of cowardice or signifies that the target isn't worth "fronting."

BANDIDO (OR BANDIT)   Someone who chases attractive young prisoners for sexual purposes.

BING   Solitary confinement.

BREAK IT DOWN   Explain it.

BURN   To take a prisoner for something; also, to masturbate while looking at a provocative picture of a woman.

CAX   Coxsackie Correctional Facility, a prison in upstate New York.

Some portions of this glossary originally appeared in an article by Howard A. Coffin in the *Philadelphia Inquirer*.

CELLIES   Cellmates.

CHICKIE   A lookout.

COMING OUT OF YOUR FACE WRONG   Bullshitting; saying stupid things.

COMING OUT THE SIDE OF YOUR NECK   Same as COMING OUT OF YOUR FACE WRONG.

CONTRACT   An agreement between prisoners, such as a "contract" to wash another prisoner's clothes in exchange for a sandwich sneaked out of the kitchen by a prisoner who works there. Prison authorities tolerate such violations because this kind of crude barter helps make prison life more tolerable for inmates.

COUNT   The roll call of prisoners. A convict is "on the count" if he is present and accounted for; hence the expression "off the count," which means (since escapes from Sing Sing and other maximum-security prisons are so rare) that a prisoner is dead, usually murdered by fellow inmates.

CREEP   Sexual offender; the lowest rung of the prison social hierarchy. Creeps never "get a hang-out card" (command enough respect to mingle and converse freely with other prisoners).

CRIMEY   A fellow prisoner who was a member of one's gang or a partner in crime.

D   A felony.

DEUCE   A couple of puffs on someone else's cigarette.

DON GEE   A big shot; "gee" is short for "gun."

DOWN   Willing.

HACK   A guard. Also known as a "roller."

HELP   Prison job. To be "on the help" means to get a prison job.

HOME PIECE   An inmate with whom one hung out before going to prison.

HOMEY   A fellow prisoner from one's neighborhood or home town.

"ISM" LANGUAGE   A black version of pig Latin.

JIG   Derogatory term for a black man.

JOHNSON (or JOHNSON RONSON, WOOD, or SWIPE)   Terms for a phallus.

KEEP-LOCK   Punish a prisoner by confining him to his cell.

KICK   Kick the habit.

KITCHEN (as in "Don't go into my kitchen without permission")   One's private life. Stems from the custom among the poor of confining guests with whom they are not on intimate terms to the living room; only intimate friends are allowed into the kitchen, where fewer pretenses can be maintained.

LAME   Sucker; chump.

LEAP SOMEONE UP   Flatter someone; to "get leaped up" can also mean to get angry.

LOCKING   As in "Where are you locking?", meaning "Where's your cell?"

LONGSHOE   Someone who's hip, slick, and "has his act together."

MELLOW-MAN   Close friend.

PA'LANTE (short for "para adelante")   Forward and onward.

PARFAIT   A young male convict who is sexually desired by fellow prisoners.

PINGÚ   Big shot; literally, "big dick."

PLEXES   Psychological complexes.

PROGRAM   The do's and don'ts of prison life. Programs are ethnically determined: they are different for whites, blacks, Puerto Ricans, etc. Programs are not enforced by prison authorities; they are determined by the prisoners themselves. The program for the whole prison population regulates the way in which members of different ethnic groups relate to one another in specific situations. It rigidly governs who sits with whom in the mess hall; where people sit in the auditorium; who smokes first; etc. It is the first thing a prisoner learns when he enters an institution. Failure to follow the program is a sure way to have trouble with fellow inmates and will result in physical reprisals— sometimes death.

RUB IT ON YOUR CHEST   Forget about it.

RUN IT   Go ahead and tell your story.

RUN IT IN THE HOLE   Do something so many times that it becomes boring; needless repetition.

SALAAM ALAIKUM (from the Arabic)   Peace be with you.

SHORT EYES   Child molester; according to prisoners, the lowest, most despicable kind of criminal.

SHORT HEIST   Any kind of pornography.

SNAKE   A homosexual.

SNAKE CHARMER   A "straight" prisoner who aggressively tries to get "snakes" to satisfy his sexual needs.

SQUEEZE   A blatant male homosexual; a queen.

STUFF   A male homosexual (not as blatant as "squeeze").

TEAROOM   Men's room, especially in subways, where homosexuals seek sexual contact with each other. To "cruise the tearoom" is to go into a men's room for homosexual purposes.

TOASTS   Long epic poems created and recited by prisoners for diversion. "Running toasts" is a favorite pastime of prisoners, and those who are good at it are likely to become popular with fellow inmates. "Standard" toasts are toasts that have been committed to memory and are still recited long after their creators are gone. Favorite standard toasts are "King Heroin," "The Ball of the Freaks," and "The Fall of the Pimp."

VAMP   Attack someone.

WIRE (as in "to put out a wire on someone")   A false rumor or untrue story.

YACOUB   White man; honky; "devil."